WAKE, SLEEPER

WAKE, SLEEPER

a memoir

೪

by
Bryan Parys

CASCADE *Books* • Eugene, Oregon

WAKE, SLEEPER
A Memoir

Cascade Books
An Imprint of Wipf and Stock Publishers
199 W. 8th Ave., Suite 3
Eugene, OR 97401

www.wipfandstock.com

ISBN 13: 978-1-4982-0786-7

Cataloguing-in-Publication Data

Parys, Bryan

Wake, sleeper: a memoir / Bryan Parys.

xvi + 172 p. ; 23 cm.

ISBN 13: 978-1-4982-0786-7

1. Biography 2. Youth 3. Evangelicalism United States I. Wake, Sleeper.

E184.P28.P20 2015

Manufactured in the U.S.A.   09/24/2015

Cover art by Jon Misarski and Tim Ferguson Sauder

For Alfred, James, Alfred James

&

Natalie

"Awake, O sleeper! Rise from the dead..."

—EPHESIANS 5:14 (NET)

"But Faith, like a jackal, feeds among the tombs, and even from these dead doubts she gathers her most vital hope."

—HERMAN MELVILLE

Contents

Author's Note

Out of respect for the various communities where the scenes from this book took place, I have changed most, but not all, names. In some cases, I have modified scene details that would otherwise easily identify the characters in question. All other content is as true as can be verified through research available to me and the lens of my memory. In the words of my mentor, Meredith Hall, "I can swear to you that this is how I've carried my story."

Permissions

PERMISSIONS

Melville, Herman, excerpt from *Moby Dick*. 1858. Public domain.

An earlier version of "Shape of a Ghost" appeared in the Summer 2012 issue of *Ruminate Magazine*.

Prologue

In Time

"A day is like a thousand years to the Lord, and a thousand years is like a day."

—2 PETER 3:8

The problem is that everything swirls.

In first grade, I am introduced to eternity. There is *in the beginning*, and there is also *world without end*. The spaces below my seat in church and the worn scoop of grass under the swing set outside are shrinking. I am inside listening to a man at the microphone say, "Christ is the One! He is it!" then I am on the playground feeling a light swipe of someone's small finger slide across my windbreaker, "You're it! You're it!" I am playing, then I am praying. If I am praying, I could also be playing. I am aging, and I believe. But I am also always doubting. I come to believe that doubting creates belief. I do not know how old I am. In the first sentence I am five; later, I am closer to now.

Now I am then.

My father dies at age thirty-eight, and I am four. The consistent message from my mother and Rick and Scott and Bob and everyone else who attends Centre Harbour Christian Fellowship with my family is: *You'll see him again. In heaven.* In heaven there is no death, only life; no time, only— what? Pure existence, or *Am*. When Moses asked God's name, He said, *I Am*. Many people try to tell me what this phrase means. Most of them try to find a word to finish God's fragment. They want, "I am *something*." They are satisfied only when God is one thing or another. If Descartes asked God's name, the answer would've echoed back: *existence*. God thinks, therefore God is. I'm supposed to think God is there, and therefore I hope I think God is here.

Time then, is a waiting. "Don't worry," Mrs. Jackson says to me in second grade, "for God, a thousand years is like one day."

"So," I say, "if God says, 'I'll end the world next week,' he means in 7,000 years?"

"Could be that long. Maybe not. The time could fly."

To grow up as a Christian means that time flies away—it exists only to show that it doesn't. When the Apostle Paul wrote a letter to a church in Thessalonica, he used the word "we" when referring to those who would be alive when Christ returned to earth. They began their frantic preparations, and so he wrote them a second letter to calm them down and explain that it *might* be them, but then, who knows?

In the 16th century, the Council of Trent closed the book on adding other books to the Bible. They decided that many of Paul's letters could be applied to any Christian, that their message would be relevant for all time— his "we" is always us, as long as we're alive. Since his words have survived, they become eternally present, constantly living in the moment because it could always be the last. Paul's moment is the moment for the woman fixing her head covering as she heard the men in Thessalonica read the newly arrived letter, the moment for the clerk who heard the Bible in English for the first time, the moment in fourth grade when I learn that John Wycliffe translated the Latin Bible into English, bringing it out of the mouths of the clergy and into the *lingua franca*, and in sixth grade when I learn that *lingua franca* means common language, or frank talk.

Let's talk frankly. I have to pee. Well, I don't now, but I did, back then. And there, I'll always have to pee, but relief will always come in the following sentence, which will really only cause you to go back to that moment where I have to pee.

In 1969, my father has to pee, and is having trouble figuring out where to find relief because he and my mother are at Yasgur's farm listening to Country Joe & the Fish. In 1973 they find relief because they have stopped growing pot in their basement window and have accepted Jesus Christ as their Lord and Savior. They are saved. Rick, Scott, Bob, and their other saved friends begin what will soon be called Centre Harbour Christian Fellowship—a nondenominational Christian church without any national funding or ties to any larger religious organization. When a railing breaks, someone in the church will secure it because they should, because they are saved and it is their turn to do the saving. When my father dies in 1987, more than one someone in the church tries to secure my mother, my little brother, my older sister, and me because they have to, because it is their turn to do the saving.

Look back—my father lives, has to pee, dies, and is in heaven. But he is not in heaven in terms of my earthly notion of *now*. His soul must wait for the Day of the Lord—but a day is a thousand; a thousand a day. The sleeping eyes of my father's soul burst open as soon as cancer closes his brown ones, and he is in heaven, because now he is outside of time. I am in second grade when I realize this for the first time—that he is already with me in heaven and we're joking about how lame earthly time is/was. In fourth grade I think about my entire existence—that everyone begins and ends in that blinking transition of my father's eternal eyes. In fifth grade, Liza dares me to go past the school boundaries, marked by a crooked, moss-covered stonewall. "Life's too short," she says.

I say, "It's already over."

I put the tip of one foot over the boundaries.

Now, we can begin.

Part One: **Static**

[**Static** *is the dots of pin-pricking sound that surround the ears when there is too much distance between the hearer and the source, the viewer and the screen, the father and the son, the Father and the Son, the heavens and the earth, the light and the dark. "In the beginning, God created the heavens and the earth," and later, "God saw that the light was good, and he separated the light from the darkness." From the beginning, it was always about separation, of the fact that you have to sleep in order to wake up and consume the crackling messages until you are too exhausted to separate the blips of language from the electric babble.*

This is the sound a memory makes: heaven and earth crossing their wires, until your eyes close again and you forget.]

1

Tape Recorder

I hear my father's voice ask, "Hi ya doin'?"

He says *hi*, but doesn't wait for a response before asking how I am doing, and so, I don't answer. He fuses the phrase because he is trying to save time. I've heard many locals around our hometown of Laconia, New Hampshire say something similar. "Hi, how ya doin'?"—then the answer, "Fine, how you?"

Everyone seems to be rushing. My mother, Barbara, is constantly moving, talking on the white phone in the kitchen, the bone-shaped receiver smudged with gray from calls that make her hands sweat. She's recently replaced the cord with a much longer one so that she can walk the length of the kitchen onto the mold-colored carpet of the dining room. From there, flipping her long brown hair behind her ear, she can look into the living room and check on my younger brother Caleb and me as we watch *Mr. Rogers*. She is talking to Mr. Chisholm, arranging what time she can drop my older sister Allyson off for the evening. Sometimes she talks to her sisters, or her mother, seeing who is free to watch us for a few hours. Other times, she is on the phone with the hospital, listening to the latest news on my father's condition. She paces the most during these calls, the snap and fall of the spiraled cord echoing off the yellow linoleum loud enough for me to hear it over the TV. It sounds like someone is playing jump rope. Following the sound, I stand between my mother and the phone base, grab the cord and start swinging it, tracing ovals in the air as the cord repeatedly smacks the floor.

My mother waves, mouthing "*Stop it.*" Her eyebrows are thick and angled as she says it, and she pushes her air-light hair out of the way so that I can see the whole picture of her annoyance. I stop swinging the cord and begin coiling it around my neck, seeing how many circles I can get. This time, she pulls the receiver away from her mouth and says, out loud, "Stop it!" Then, moving the phone back, she says to Mr. Chisholm, "Listen, I have to go. We have to get going."

When she hangs up the cord spins itself into an infinity of loops, and she is moving me, telling me to get ready to go while she packs us some toys. We are out the door, and we are almost running.

My father, Alfred Parys, is barely moving in his hospital bed. Esophageal cancer has weakened his grip when I hold his hand, and his voice sounds like a radio station that is losing signal. There is static in his room when we are not there because my father speaks into a black and gray tape recorder. "Hey family," he says into the crackling blackness. "Hi ya doin'?" He is losing time. There is not enough left for the "how."

I cannot answer his question because I am listening to the tape shortly after his death. He seems to know this and does not pause before continuing. He addresses each of his three children individually, his sentences ending early because his breath is having a hard time keeping up. Caleb is just two years old, and my dad says, "It will be harder for him to. Well, probably easier for him to see. To adjust. But in time he'll. Understand." Caleb will not remember anything about what's happening, but later, he can hear his father ask him how he is doing.

He tells me that, being the oldest male, I'll have a bit more to take on. "You don't have to worry about being the complete man of the house, because Jesus will take that spot. A lot of the weight of the man of the house will be on your shoulders." Here, his sentences break down again, scattering as he tries to put a future he won't see into words. "As the years go on. As you get older. Your role will get bigger. And. I know you'll do very well. Because you're a good boy. Like Caleb is. You're all good children."

I want to rewind, back to when we were miming small talk, but it is always followed by having to fast-forward past the part about me.

As I listen, a tightness forms in my throat and spreads outward to a ring around my neck like a noose, a yoke. I have a job, and that job has me by the throat. Later in the tape, when my dad is speaking his thoughts on faith as they come to him, he says, paraphrasing Scripture, that, "If you know Jesus. Then you're as close to the Father as you can be."

I know Jesus, and I knew my father, and now I'm as close to being a father as I can be.

There are still a couple weeks left of preschool, and despite my protestations to my mother that I need to stay home and take care of things, she insists that she'll be fine and that I should go. "It'll only be a few hours, and then I'll come pick you up and you can take care of me again. How about this: I'll wash your Robin pajamas so you can wear them again tonight."

"Can I wear the cape to bed?"

"Absolutely not. It'll wrap around your neck in the middle of the night and suffocate you."

"Hey everyone. Look who it is: *Karate Kid*," Jeff Shawmut says soon after my mom drops me off at Jack and Jill Nursery School, a brick building next to the local Catholic church. I don't have many friends here, and I am mostly preoccupied with getting back to the house under the abstract auspices of "needing to take care of things." A few weeks ago, hoping to make a friendly connection, I had made small talk with Jeff and told him how much I like *Karate Kid* and that I hoped to get lessons soon. "Hey Daniel-*san*! Why don't you do some kicks for us?" he continues, making sure everyone in the playroom can hear.

I try to ignore him and walk through the back door, out to the hallway, but he and his friends follow. At the end of the hall, they pin me against the back entrance door, grab the string from the Venetian blinds covering its window, and tie it around my neck until I can't breathe.

At the end of the day I walk out the door to meet Mom at our faded white Bronco, she gives me a hug, pauses, and says, "Why's your neck all red, honey?" Without much of an explanation, she runs back into the building yelling at Mrs. Morin and demanding to know why they didn't do the obvious thing and call her immediately. During the drive home, she is visibly frustrated, wondering why the teachers didn't say anything. "I don't understand it anymore than you do," she says.

I'm starting to get used to the splinters. Every day, after the copper cow bell rings to signal the end of lunch time, the first-through-fourth graders line up by class, abandoning games of Girls-Chase-Boys or Boys-Chase-Girls. On our teacher's signal, my first-grade classmates and I march through the dark brown elementary building of Laconia Christian School, past the first grade room and out the back door to the woodshed, arms out, ready to be stacked blind with pitchy pine logs for the woodstoves that heat each classroom.

Some of the fourth graders stay behind and clean the bathrooms while the rest of us stock the wood-boxes. There are no janitors here, and no maintenance staff, so all the students pitch in to keep things in order. I carry my five or six pine wedges into the yellow-painted first-grade room, and slide them noisily into the rough-sawn pine box lining the back of the room. Splinters stop scaring me after a few months, and most of us figure out how to remove them, since there is no school nurse on duty—because there is no school nurse.

On my father's tape, he says that there are times when we can act like children, but there will be more and more times where we will have to be more grown up.

During chore time, the teachers talk to us like coworkers: "Can you take one more?" "Hold on, lemme grab the door." I am one of them, bearing the same caretaking burdens.

After the box has been refilled, I watch as Mrs. Doucette turns the squeaky, coiled handle and opens the stove's side door, releasing smoke that will come to permeate our Bible workbooks. She grabs a few logs from the box and heaves them in, sparks skittering, embers popping in a fiery cloud from the hot heart. For now, she is being practical, parental.

When the door clasps shut, she turns, and school is back in session.

I pick the last of the dangling strands of bark out of my sleeves, and take out a piece of dotted line paper, rip a clean corner, and start eating it.

Mrs. Doucette never catches me eating paper. I let a sheaf of paper hang out of my desk and rip Chiclet-sized pieces without taking my eyes off of her. I lay another piece on my tongue and let the saliva slowly soak it through before chewing it to a wadded pulp, swirling the fibers on my tongue.

Our paperboy and his family are moving to Illinois this summer, shortly after my sixth birthday. I have always liked the orange-sashed shoulder bag that Aaron carries his bundle of news in, so I ask if I can have it. My mom, new stepdad James, and Aaron all take this as a request to enter the working world; I can't think of any reasons why not, so I start going on the twenty-four-house route with Aaron in order to learn the ropes.

"Friday is collection day," he teaches me. "You have to knock on each door and ask for their money. The LaPentas usually leave an envelope in the mailbox, so theirs is usually the easiest."

My mother remarried shortly after I turned six, and Caleb and I immediately went from calling him Jim to Dad. Allyson continues to call him Jim. A Vietnam vet and Frito-Lay route manager, he is quiet, calm, having already lived through the noise of war and raising a son on his own. His first wife had a child with someone else, and my dad adopted him as his own. When they divorced, he got custody, and raised him alone. He is not new to the selfless game of love.

"This is your paybook," my new dad explains as Aaron hands down his canvas bag and money pouch. "Every Saturday morning you'll sit with me at the table and I'll do my bills, and you'll do yours. You've got to make sure everyone pays on time."

The pay comes by way of tips, if the customer feels like it. Most weeks, I end up with 75 cents and an occasional lipstick-stained Charleston Chew.

Each weekday afternoon, I ride my scooter down the cracked sidewalk, a bass-driven theme song that I make up pounding in my head. On one afternoon a few months in, the front wheel of the scooter catches a crack in front of the LaPenta's house, and I fly forward over the handlebars, skinning my left knee. Rolling over, I examine the abrasion, and it looks like a ghost. Blood beads around the edges, gathers at the ghost's mouth, and drools down my shin and onto my plastic flip-flop. The words of work from my fathers collect in my head, and instead of running home and getting Mom to spray it with the stinging mist of Bactine, I lift my bleeding leg up and climb the stairs to deliver the paper. As I speed away, the wind cools and dries the trickle of blood in its track.

On Saturday mornings before heading out on the route, I sit at the dining room table with my worn paybook open to the current week, and I scan for unchecked boxes—those who haven't yet paid. My dad sits opposite me with statements, bills, and a rainbow-hued coffee mug surrounding him. He lifts his head frequently, the perfectly round bald spot in the middle of his head rising as he looks through the bottom half of his glasses while he makes checks out.

"How many missing this week?" he asks without looking up at me, as if we were partners at a collection agency.

"Two," I answer. "I mean . . . four."

He looks up now, his hands pausing their shuffling and folding.

"Did you knock on their doors yesterday?"

"Yes. I mean no. I mean, the Fraziers weren't home. I think."

"You have a duty to your employer to account for every cent. You can't let people get away with not paying."

Keep an account—I am to collect, and also to track what is lost, what I'm losing.

I am terrified of knocking on doors. When anyone answers, their faces always suggest that they don't owe me anything. *We didn't sign up for this part of the deal* it looks like. Sometimes I stand on the steps for ten minutes, my hand raised but motionless. When I knock it feels like a kind of unwanted divination—that I'm always interrupting something grave. I listen for movement, for the placing or dropping of something metallic, a click like hitting a pause button, and hear the muted slap of slippers on linoleum, onto the stunted shag of the living room, getting closer, closer. On the occasions when no one answers, I think for some reason that it is my fault. It is as if they are waiting for the right person to call them back to the world, and they know it's not the kid waiting for his $2.75.

Still, when I hear no sound from the other side, a great weight leaves my chest. I run down and hop on my scooter before they realize that perhaps that noise that was haunting them was someone knocking.

"You have to be more thorough, bud," he says. "You can't let yourself get distracted from your work."

Two years after I start, the route grows to thirty-two houses, and it seems that I am always getting distracted. The second-to-last house is swarmed with bees that hover over a crumbling cement walkway. Bees and hornets scare me to death. On my third birthday, before my father is sick, I climb a slide in our side yard, and my foot nudges a papery nest that is stuck to the handrail. Inky black dots dart past, towards my eyes, and I scream, almost losing my balance, until my dad rushes over and scoops my whole frame up, running me into the house. My mother fills a bucket with ice and places it in the tub as my dad spins me around and dunks my head into the numbing cold.

Even though he is only four, I start making Caleb come with me on my route. Somehow, he is not fazed by the bees at all, delivering the paper to its prescribed spot without ever breaking his calm gait. But my father Alfred knew that things would be easier for him, because he didn't understand what was going on. He doesn't remember or know that death flies past our eyes whenever we try to move ahead with the practical tasks laid before us each day—he cannot hear the buzzing that rewinds, distracts me from taking the next step forward.

Years later, after a Thanksgiving meal that leaves us all tryptophanned and nostalgic, I say to Allyson: "Remember when I hit that hornets' nest when we lived on Jefferson Street?"

"That didn't happen to you; that happened to me. That's why I'm scared to death of bees."

"No, that's why *I'm* scared to death of bees," I say. "Mom, who got stung by all those hornets over at the old house?"

"Someone got stung over at Jefferson Street? I don't remember anything like that." Caleb was only one when it happened, and now Alfred is not here to confirm which version is true.

The tape my father leaves is 00:24:46 long. Each year, I push the button marked with two left-facing arrows, listening to the screeching reverse of ribbon and time until it starts over from the beginning. Every time, he examines his future and deals with his bleak prognosis, never intoning the word *death*, but instead referring to the probable outcome as "the obvious thing." It is a contradiction—something being obvious but unnamed. Amidst last thoughts for his family and concise ruminations on a faith he believes in more than ever, he deviates to the mundane. "I am just testing the voice-activated mechanism," he says. He is being practical, day-to-day, as if he is at work. *Voice-activated mechanism* are generally not words for your last days, but here they are, preserved between a cough and a click of the thick red button. They are three more words I can add to my father's lexicon. No matter how many times I listen, I can never add *death*.

I rewind this moment over and over, dwelling in the one instance where my father is normal, like everyone around me who is thinking about working, about how things work, not about when they will die. Being normal is being distracted from death. Right now, I am abnormal.

There is a warp in the tape, then another click, then the static sounds that signify that things are being recorded. But here, my father does not speak. There is a TV on in the background, a man's voice saying, "For the first time in fifty years—" then he is cut off by the sound of my mother talking on the phone by my father's hospital bed. She is talking to a friend, a sister maybe. Allyson is at the Chisholm's, and it is a school night for her, so my mother is trying to figure out when she can get over there to pick her up. "The boys," she says, are somewhere else, and she has packed toys for them that they don't normally play with. "Maybe they'll think they're new," she says laughing, but the sound decays quickly. Caleb and I are not there because, as my dad has said elsewhere on the tape, we tend to run around too much. In a hospital, with our father barely able to push a button, my brother and I inadvertently figure out a way to run away from him.

The TV and my mother battle for space on the tape. When she pauses, the documentarian's voice answers her, most of the time in full phrases, as if my mom has planned it out like a conversation. He is talking about King Tut's tomb. It is 1987—fifty-five years ago, in 1922, Howard Carter discovered the long-lost, treasure-laden tomb of King Tutankhamen, the pharaoh famous for taking over his father's duties at age nine, and then dying only nine years later. He was as close to a father as he could be.

Was my father aware of the parallels? Is this why he didn't say a word during this section of the tape? Or, was he making another attempt at normalcy in the face of his obvious thing, recording an elongated period of ambient sounds that spoke of family logistics and ancient Egypt, and because of their juxtaposition, connecting them through history into a tiny plastic spool of film?

The documentarian is talking about the wonder of the tomb, and how it is not always available to the touring public. The more people cast their eyes on the glory of Tut's burial adornments, the more the tomb is in danger of disintegration. Within the temple, he says, "thoughts inevitably turn towards—." My mother interrupts him this time, talking again, so I have to rewind the tape a few times, cranking the volume to hear his obvious word: *destruction.*

He goes on saying, "Paradoxically, the vibrations caused by the footsteps of the tourists who visit each year, even the carbon dioxide they exhale, are eroding the irreplaceable treasures."

By rewinding and stretching the tape, am I eroding his audio tomb? It feels greedy to reenter this sonic sarcophagus whenever I forget what my father sounds like, frightened by how the timbre of our voices are synthesizing more and more each time I return.

In 1922, in the last year of the project's funding and with his job on the line, Howard Carter tapped through a wall in the Valley of Kings that soon proved to be the place he'd been searching for.

"Can you see something?" he was asked as he put a candle through the hole and looked in, centuries of hot air breathing on him, choking him into silence.

"Yes. Wonderful things," he finally pushed out. His work paid off.

When Tut reaches his obvious thing, his people fill his room with wonderful things that, for hundreds of years become lost, hidden things. Through Carter's candle, they become wonderful again. Fifty-five years later, my father's tape is ending, just as Tut's tomb is inevitably in danger of due to the increase of steps, coughs, hands that want to touch, to not let go, to endlessly compare then and now, now and forever.

[**Static** *is the sound discipline makes—the abrupt and piercing shock from touching something you shouldn't, from thinking you are alone, not knowing there is someone in leather slippers sliding over a shag carpet behind you, waiting to touch you with a slap of paternal, spine-straightening energy. It buzzes through the air like a fly that has flown where it shouldn't, after it was told to get out, get out, you're not supposed to be in here, before receiving an open-palmed smack. But it is also the sound of healing. In Luke 7, when a sick woman pushes through a crowd and touches her finger to the cloak of Jesus, she is immediately healed by a spark of the divine. "'Who touched me?' Jesus asked. When they all denied it, Peter said, 'Master, the people are crowding and pressing against you.' But Jesus said, 'Someone touched me; I know that power has gone out from me.'" The static touch takes power away, but you don't know why.*]

2

Discipled

1

The smell is of burnt dust. The tiny particles spark and fuse with the electricity scuffed from the thin carpet, stinging the linings of my nose. Squinting, I see molecules floating past the window behind the dark brown hair of my kindergarten teacher, Mrs. Orr. She stands in front of me with a supinated palm, saying something about this not hurting, at least not as much as it will her. Is she next? When I leave, will she ask herself to bend over her knee, praying to God for forgiveness before twisting herself into a paddled pretzel?

We are in Dr. Smith's office, though in my six months as a kindergartener at Laconia Christian School, I've never seen the man or woman to whom the moniker belongs. Though no one has confirmed the gender, the office feels masculine, haunted by an electric ghost of discipline from years of spankings carried out in this room. I assume that this was Dr. Smith's office at one time, and for some reason, his legacy has remained, the mere utterance of the name causing a shock of pain through our overalls.

While it is called an office, it is hardly more than a broom closet, which, when not hosting disobedient children, is its primary function. The walls are lined with books—ones that are so thick and faded they might as well be carved into place, their grain worn and full of splinters. There is one chair and, behind that, an old Electrolux vacuum like the one my mother has, only browner and more prehistoric. There are only two reasons why any student would be in here: to get the vacuum, or to get spanked.

It is an abnormally cold morning in February, in the sense that it is always this cold in February, but it never feels normal. At its bitter peak, winter in New Hampshire goes through three stages—December is full of lights and evergreens, January of incomprehensible snow banks that allow you to only see what is directly in front of you, and February a windless chill that leaves the air so still, the sound of dirt underfoot echoes across a parking lot like the shot of an old Winchester.

As soon as my classmate Melanie and I stepped off the bus this morning, the cold was on us. Without the wind to move it, the air clings to you, drying and cracking the seams of our eyelids until shutting them feels like ripping stitches.

"I'm really cold," Melanie says through a double-wrapped scarf, her breath forming a wet circle over the same spot on her scarf as I breathe into on mine. She is clutching a *Smurfs* lunch box with a hand stuck in a mitten, the other hand buried in a faded parka.

"We're not supposed to go inside until the bell," I muffle, stating the rule but not understanding it.

"We're gonna freeze if we stay out here."

We go inside, believing it is good and right.

The last instruction Christ gave to his followers was to create more followers: "Go make disciples." One of the first things he said as an adult was, "Come, follow me." Before ever using the word *disciple*, he implied its definition, and left everyone else to piece it together.

Discipline, it seems to me, is to make someone a disciple, to make someone follow you, or at least follow the person that you are trying to follow.

When we turn into the kindergarten room, on the ground level of what is also the middle school building, Mrs. Orr is sitting at her desk, somehow already staring at us in disbelief.

"You're not supposed to be in here until the bell," she says.

"We know," I begin, hoping to talk our way out of this.

"Well, that's disobedience, and you know by now what that means." She gets up and walks past us, the perfumed breeze that rushes after her carries a weight like a tipped scale as it brushes against our noses, and we inhale the sin-sense, internalizing the guilt that follows it.

So, I am in Dr. Smith's office because I am cold.

Then, I bend like a drinking bird over her pleated lap and the cakey smell of her make-up becomes an anesthetic to the hand that is raised and dropped into a slap over my corduroyed butt. No sooner does the blow fall than her hand rises again, this time to wrap around me and meet her other hand, creating the pose of a prayerful hug. As she prays forgiveness for me her eyes moisten at the slits, and through the lessening sting underneath my pants, I wonder why she puts herself through this. Up to this point she had been in such stern control that it seemed she was waiting at her desk for someone to go rogue and come inside prematurely. But now she has gone soft, the hug is motherly, open, and defeated. The prayer seems like a veiled apology. I look up at her and accept it, the pain fading as I watch her back slump, each prayed phrase deconstructing into pleading incoherence: *And help Bryan . . . me . . . help . . . . Help us . . . . Amen.*

"Please tell Melanie to come in," she musters, shaking off the penitence as I leave, walking carefully, the scent of dust and static clinging to my whole body. I have already started to forget the pain, but the charred warmth of Dr. Smith's office will remain for much, much longer.

The woodstove in the first-grade classroom keeps us warm. Throughout each day, its heat is provoked, the large black lips pried open to force-feed it dry wedges carried in from the neat, re-puzzled stacks in the woodshed. Settling in for afternoon classes, the students remove their boots and slide into the slippers that wait in a staple-shaped arrangement around the thick breath of the stove, replacing them with the boots that will be crisp-dried by the day's last bell. I slide my hand into one of the slippers, pushing my fingers over the toe-worn depressions arcing at the tip. Lifting it, I examine the sole—dusty white plastic stippled with treads, some near the toes still sharply rounded, others by the heel rubbed to the essence of circles. I press the sole to the side of the stove and a sizzle of brown smoke causes me to yank it back, leaving a horseshoe imprint, dotted with the pinhole scars from the textured bottom. Its stain is stark and rotten, the white caramelizing into shit brown, and yet no one has seen what I've done. I shove my foot into the slipper, the splinters of guilt starting in my toes like hot sulfur.

Before we settle in for class, our first-grade teacher, Mrs. Doucette, calls out my best friend Brian Greene, her eyes pointing at him from behind her wire rims, and I can tell just from the look that Dr. Smith is waiting for him. When he returns from the office, I am surprised at how all *that* only took a few minutes. He walks to the front of the class, a no-teeth smile hanging below the padding of his combed blond hair. He stops at the blackboard and bounces his butt off the wall a few times before sitting at his desk.

Why is he smiling?

Is he telling us that what we all know just happened didn't hurt, and see, isn't he brave? Or is it because he feels the guilt too, the guilt that he has done something he just barely knows is wrong—can't explain the error, but now can feel it, can really feel it—and his smile says hey, I've learned my lesson but the rest of you haven't; you'll be up here smiling soon and something about you will be different—the way you think about yourself, your every movement when other eyes are on you, that smell of electric dust burning from outside, inside, covering you in a film that will not come off in the bathtub, or dried away with a towel, but will be a stain that you can't see—you will be introduced to pain?

The traditional translation of Proverbs 22:6 begins, "Train up a child in the way he should go, and when he is old, he will not depart from it." The *should* of course implying the set of doctrines within which the proverb appears. *Train* seems appropriate here—like it is a montage in a *Rocky* movie. Through hard work, one will achieve the life desired. Another translation stiffens things up a bit and replaces *Train* with *Direct*. Where a training coach is on the sidelines, directing feels more hands-on, like someone is behind you, making you walk somewhere so that you are less focused on your own biology, and rather more on that tensed, determined grip digging into your shoulders. There is no thought as to where you are headed and it makes any kind of arrival feel impossible.

✕

We are teaching ourselves how to do a split. The woodstove in the second-grade classroom we are sprawled around breathes and the wood pops, causing the warp of sheet metal to thud off the walls of the room. Liza, Melanie, Brian Greene, Paul Howard, and I are stretching our legs as far as they will go, testing the elasticity of tendon, the corners of our eyes squinting downward to meet the upturned peaks of our mouths. The tightness in my groin feels like it will pull to the point of fraying at any moment, but I push it, bringing the pain on myself in regimented increments.

"My aerobics instructor showed me these stretches," Melanie says, her brown ponytail held by neon clips and draping down the front of her shirt as she bows her head into the full body stretch she is attempting. "She says if you do this for two weeks, every day, anyone can do a split whenever they want."

Liza's translucent pink glasses slide down her nose as she looks up and concentrates on bringing her thigh closer to the ash-stained brown-and-tan carpet, mouthing *owowow* as she breathes in and out. "Man," she says. "This takes discipline!"

Her last word perches on her pale lips, as she readies herself for pain— pain that is supposedly good, correctional. I do not have the patience to do this for two weeks, so I try to fast-forward by plying the taffy-muscle in one quick jerk. *Geeaughh*, I say, my legs bouncing instinctively back to a normal position as I fall sideways onto the carpet, feeling the tracked-in pebbles and bark bits press themselves into my cheek.

On the other side of the room Adam is finishing the string cheese that Aarim had tried trading his whole lunch for, and with that, Mrs. Pollack announces in her calm, watery way, "Ok—you may all head out for recess."

The exercises quickly fade into a cave of memory as we bolt outside. Pulling a spring jacket over his shirt that makes him look like a blond Charlie Brown, Brian looks at me and whispers "*sing it*" as we head out the door.

"Teen wolf," I begin muttering slow and low, and then in gradual chromatic tones I repeat our version of the theme song of the Saturday morning cartoon we've only seen commercials for. "Teen wolf / Teen wolf / Teen teen teen teen te-en wolf." Brian's teeth are seething, and his shoulders rise and fall with the increasing pace of the song, the muscles in his face pumping, turning the outlines of his eyes red until we both scream and run through the dirt parking lot, crashing into each other, canine claws flying and grasping at the rocks underfoot.

There is a lump of quartz sitting under a picnic table in the middle of the playground. It looks precious, expensive, and I don't believe it when friends tell me I can't get money for finding them, so I slip it into my pocket. Brian picks up a jagged peach-pit-sized piece of granite, jumps up on the picnic table, and with a guttural yell, flings it at a rusting garbage can about twenty-five feet away. Liza and Melanie have strolled our way, and are standing a few feet to the right of the can, laughing and speaking in a girls-only language they call "Gibberish."

"Te-thuh-gee te-thuh-gye," Liza says, her eyes shifting back and forth towards Brian and Melanie.

"Te-thuh-goo!" Melanie cackles back, neither of them able to resist the hilarious weight of their covert exchange.

Brian chucks another stone that slaps the side of the can with a ping and bounces sharp left. For good luck, I take the quartz out, rolling it in my palm like dice as I eye the mouth of the can. Brian misses the receptacle entirely this time, and I can picture myself heaving the perfect toss, an obedient arc that lands in the bottom center of the can, right in plain view of the girls. They'll look at me and giggle shyly. I bring my arm back and step into the throw like my stepdad has shown me in T-ball practice. The glimmering bone-white shard flicks the right lip-edge of the metal and slices its way through the brown strands on Melanie's head. Her screaming is as instantaneous as the blood that pours out, as if it was just waiting for the opportunity to be released.

I am shuddering at the stained quartz by her feet, at the tiny droplets gathering and sliding down to the tips of her pony tail, at the teacher running, then teachers, then Brian running away, then someone taking Melanie, then me alone, shuddering for a few more seconds before Mr. Glasier turns and says, "Bryan! Inside! Now!"

Another proverb that is much more often quoted than the one about training or directing children is earlier in Proverbs 13, and seems to define the "direct" method by recommending the use of hands. When people repeat it in conversation, they often only say the first few words, tilting their eyes up sternly, telling the other person that they may be going too soft on their progeny. "Spare the rod . . ." they say, the eyes adding the ellipsis. The reason for self-editing is pretty clear when you hear the rest of the verse: "Those who spare the rod hate their children." Ellipsis eyes become a way to accuse the party in question of hating their kids while omitting the actual accusation.

The second half of the verse gives the converse of the first, in good proverbial fashion, but it leaves out the mention of the rod, and cleverly throws in a word that will forever be associated with hands-on direction: "Those who love their children care enough to *discipline* them." Psalm 32 calls it "the hand of discipline," even. If you love your kids, you'll keep your hand on them until they start walking in the right direction.

Mrs. Pollack, Mr. Glasier, and Mrs. Doucette are talking, almost out of earshot while I sit and wait in a plastic chair. I can't believe how stupid I was, that someone called an ambulance because I just had to throw that perfect piece of quartz. The metal legs on the chair are triangles that connect back to front. I lift the front end by leaning back, then push my left foot under it and depress the weight in full on the joint edge where foot meets toe. Veins thump, and I overhear snippets, something about Melanie and staples. As if they are taking turns their heads look over at me, one at a time—Doucette, Glasier, Pollack, repeat.

"Well, I'm not sure he needs *that*," Mrs. Pollack says, her face oaken and frowning.

"He certainly does!" says Mr. Glasier, spiking the volume of their discussion. "We've told them a hundred times not to throw rocks because someone is bound to get hurt." His dark mustache somehow remains fixed as his head shakes and his eyelids flit as if he is malfunctioning.

"I'll do it," Mrs. Doucette adds with confidence.

"But it was just an accident—what can you do? They're both already pretty shaken up as it is," says Mrs. Pollack, her palms up in supplication, less like she is defending my cause, and more like she is pleading with them: *don't spank him.*

"No," says Mr. Glasier. "I'll do it." He looks at me, his small eyes approaching me, and his lids still flipping like a hummingbird. He motions for me to follow him and we move in the direction of Dr. Smith's. "You know who this hurts more," he says, but in this case, I can't help but think that it's Melanie who's in the most pain. I wonder if he will try to inflict something that will resemble what Melanie felt as the quartz found its way into her skull—must his slap match the sin? If it doesn't, is Melanie some-how wronged further?

He keeps talking and blinking and not wriggling his mustache as he turns his hand into a paddle. The *thwack* lands on my jeans, and the noise startles me. I realize that this is the only thing that gives me pause. It doesn't hurt at all. I look up at his face; it slacks low then snaps into pained place as he raises his hand again. It drops fast, but slows on impact. He seems startled at my silence and I wonder if he thinks it's out of insolence. He is just waiting for me to make a sound so this can finally, please, stop.

"Ow."

The tightness around his jaw releases at the sound, and he shakes his paddle-hand out, folding it into prayer, saying "Oh God, help us."

I walk out with a sad smile tucked under my lips, at the weakness of his hand, at the fact that maybe this actually does hurt him more than me—why do they do this to themselves? I breathe in long and slow, a sacred cake of dust cracking off my limbs, its scent leaving me, the second skin discarded as chastised chaff on the threshing floor of Dr. Smith's office.

"Did you learn something from all this?" he asks, the lids tripping, but slower.

"Uh-huh."

$$\times$$

But there's something more to Psalm 32 beyond that disciplining hand. In verse nine, the psalmist, King David in this case, puts God's words in his mouth and says, "Do not be like a senseless horse or mule that needs a bit and bridle to keep it under control." You wouldn't call your bound horse your disciple, right? You're not teaching it anything except that there will be odd moments when it'll try to move forward, or try to say something, and you'll violently tug on its gums until it shuts up and does something different.

2

In seventh-grade science, we have been learning about insects, and our big project for the chapter is an annotated chart of bugs we are to collect and pin with our own thumbs and pointer fingers. My project isn't going so well. With less than a week to go before the due date, I have a half-gutted cricket and an almost-unidentifiable silverfish. Unlike most of the twelve-year-old boys in my class, my hands are not the type to pick up neon salamanders by their wriggling tails, or even let admittedly cute woolly caterpillars crawl like renegade eyebrows up my forearm.

As I begin spelunking behind the eight-foot cubes of prickly hedges in the front of my house, I soon find that I scamper as wildly as the bugs do when we meet eye to compound eye. I do not have the patience and steady hand that I've seen my classmates Paul, Andrew, or Levi employ when crouching on their haunches, their fingers grappling like an arcade skill crane around the abdomen of a grasshopper, its legs kicking fast and cyclically, not yet realizing that the world has been turned upside down.

I breathe in deep and exhale quickly, resolving to turn over the rock at my foot and collect whatever lurks beneath. Bending down, the acrid smell of cloistered dirt getting closer and more concentrated, I push at a semi-submerged lump of granite. Cracks form and widen at its sides, a stagnant breath blowing out. It keeps slipping, forcing me to go after it with two hands, cupping and prying at the clean topside, and then smudging my fingers on the exhumed earth of the rock's dusty, lower stratum.

While my hands hold up the stone, black dots run in all directions but straight. They are overcome by madness because they have been left to their own devices. "If I could just get my hands on one," I think, but I'm weighted down by holding up the rock. So, inert, I just watch as dozens of wild things go wherever they want. I crouch and put my back into rolling the stone away to the side, a tingling crick sliding up my spine. By the time I've rested it next to the hole, all the bugs are gone. It doesn't matter that they had no leader, that their scuttling often looked circular, crooked, wrong—they still escaped and they still have their whole lives in front of them.

By hand-in time at the end of the week I've added a beetle and a grasshopper, both of which have been partially dissected by the tread on my Nikes. I am astonished by the other projects—all have reached the ten-insect minimum, some have mounted each insect with pins onto sanded pine frames that open and close on a hinge, others have typed out the scientific and common names, each wholly intact specimen shining like it was on loan from the garden of Eden's entomology department. Mine is a reused manila folder with each bug squashed into place by craft tape that at least holds the grasshopper's dangling leg in place. I have written just their common names below each one in Bic pen. When I bring it up front to Mrs. Carey, she informs me that the silverfish is actually a house centipede, and is, therefore, not even an insect. In vain, I argue for half credit, saying that it is a rare find, concealing the fact that when I found it, it was already dead and desiccated.

So, she peruses my folder, having difficulty opening it due to dried gut spots, mutters something, then looks up at me through her long, wavy black hair, a lightning strike of white down the front, and I can tell I've taken a wrong turn somewhere.

Disciple shares roots with discipline, but its connotations are far more positive, in that it suggests someone who can follow just fine on their own, hands free. Its Latin root is *discipulus*, meaning learner or pupil. But both words are inextricably bridled to religion due to their uses in the Jewish Scriptures (in the Psalms, Proverbs), the Christian Bible (Jesus' twelve disciples), and the various sects and cults that followed for centuries after, self-flagellating, correcting, and disciplining themselves into apt pupils. Discipline creates disciples, for sure, but it also etches indelible ink marks on those that don't understand what they're being turned into, their self-transformations triggered secondhand.

There is a chart above Mrs. Carey's desk in our seventh-grade room with a fluctuating series of colored marks next to the names of the seventeen kids in my class. The marks graph the moments where we are not following Mrs. Carey. The colors showcase the severity of your misstep, breaking down as follows:

- Yellow: standing up without permission
- Red: talking out of turn
- Brown: making fun of a classmate
- Black: disrespecting the teacher

Three marks in any combination of red, yellow or brown means an after-school detention. One black equals one detention. Since the list is alphabetical, I can tell from halfway across the room how sinful my classmates have been this week, watching their disobedience grow like a mechanical horse race at a carnival. Currently, I am this bad: one red, one yellow (||).

It seems I have been having a hard time keeping quiet. Mrs. Carey is teaching something, and because she teaches us all subjects except for math, the concepts are borderless, hard to hold onto. I am sitting with my hands resting on my desk, a desk that when I look down at it demands me to assess its condition in my head: the glossy, fake-wood panel is peeling on the left corner. Should I raise my hand and tell the teacher my desk is breaking? Or is this an example of what she means when she tells me that I'm getting lost in details that don't matter? Look back up—don't get lost again.

Tommy French is smirking under the cover of his sandy red hair, a buck knife splayed open in his hands and carving a pencil just inside his desk. Go on; add your commentary: there are flecks of yellow snowing onto his sneaker and the rust-colored carpet below him, Mrs. Carey's voice peaking and diving. His chart for the week: more black marks than anyone. The room is alive with his quiet tension, a nervous anger that needs to be put into words. But we mustn't *talk back*—a phrase that means, according to Mrs. Carey, that when we want to respond, that urge is out of something rebellious, unchecked. So Tommy flays a pencil, dismembering a tool of words into stifled fragments. I look away, and Ruth's graphite hair is fanned in strands over her desk—which is not peeling—her neck craned slightly to the left, suggesting that she is drawing something. Art, she calls it; stop doodling, says Mrs. Carey. I want to look at what she is making, but that would require standing without permission, meaning: |. Number of Ruth's marks this week: 0.

My friend Andrew's thin, parted blond hair dips around the crown of his head—an impression left by the tie-dye bandana he was wearing during break that Mrs. Carey told him to remove because it was a sign of rebellion. She thinks about the color of rebellion, and tells him to put up a red mark. Andrew and I dressed up as hippies for a Halloween party at our classmate Jeff's house this year, and that seemed to bother a lot of the parents and teachers around us. So much so that the party ended early because Jeff's mom called our parents saying the sight of us, "all sticking together in the back corner," made them and Jeff's little sister uncomfortable.

"They look like we did thirty years ago," I overheard his mother say to her husband. We brought something back to them, evidently, a vision of what it used to be like, BC, before *their* Christ, and it scared the hell back into them. When my dad had to drive forty-five minutes to pick us all up three hours early, he said, "You look ridiculous, bud. Funny, maybe, but not scary."

Since then, we have started wearing a hippie item or two to school, reveling in our ability to jog memories, letting them remember that we follow them, but that sometimes that means that we follow older versions of them. To us, it is a costume, but they see bell-bottomed ghosts sneaking out of their brain closets, parading their pasts they had hoped would stay forgotten after converting to Christianity.

I keep a peace necklace tucked under my collar and pull it out during recess. When Mrs. Carey caught me with it last week, she told me to remove it. "That's an upside-down broken cross," she said. A few days later, a student from the high school visited our class and spoke to us about the dangers of cult symbols such as the peace sign and the yin-yang. The coolness of the pendant against my bare sternum quietly morphs into something branding, marking me as one who does not follow.

For years I have been filled with discipleship. The word *discipline* is used when you're bad, *disciple* when you're good. I do not bring a knife to school, but I sneak in peace, and somehow I know I feel guiltier about my transgression than Tommy does about his whittling wiles.

We learn more about insects. Proboscis, abdomen, antennae: sucker, armor, feelers—feelers that are always searching for something. I want to raise my hand, stand up straight like we are taught to, and point to a fly that is trapped in between the screen and the window, its buzzing volume increasing every time it hits the wire mesh. For me, it is an unending distraction that says *speak, speak*. I want to convey with the clearest elocution that the fly looks like it is incapable of following any path because it can't find the ground, that it is flitting back and forth to make up for this fact, until something outside opens and lets him out. The drone is constant—it has to create sound—getting louder only when it realizes it's wrong, trapped, dead wrong. But their noise is simply the beating of wings, an echo of seeming aimlessness, the volume rising when attempts at stasis are continually halted.

The slapping of my thoughts against Mrs. Carey's lecture is so disorienting that I look up at the ceiling tiles that resemble Frosted Mini-Wheats and cross my eyes until the edges of the white segments blur. Paul partly rises out of his seat and leans over to blow on the paper snowflake dangling by a thread of yarn over Ruth's desk.

"Paul," says Mrs. Carey, "Please put up a yellow mark." Marks Paul has as he walks like a senseless mule towards the chart: ||. Marks he has when he walks back: ||| = detention.

I am still staring upward; Mrs. Carey is still teaching. "Insects breathe through tiny holes called spiracles that lead to their respiratory systems." I bite my lip to keep myself from singing, "All I need is a spiracle / All I need is you." I picture it as sung by a grounded but injured fly, its half-crushed carapace blocking its breathing, its wings smashed silent. The song is its chart-topping death lament.

"If you look in your book at the diagram of the katydid—"

"KATIE DID WHAT?" I say, much louder than I expect, surprised by the words that have fallen out, tugged on by the unwavering lure of a pun, of the fact that a word can mean two things, maybe more.

"Bryan, please—" she says, like glass breaking and letting everything, everyone, thank God, fly out in a hundred directions at once.

[**Static** *is the act of not acting, or thinking that standing still amidst fluttering specters will create peace. But it can also be the friction of your feet against the ground, of your clothes against your moving body, running away from a problem—but the static doesn't have to move to catch up to you in the middle of the night. "A problem." That is, the ending. Movement is a myth that you've created to symbolize change.*]

3

Hyssop Tag

1

The grey metal folding chairs tilt and dig into the rocky sand of Centre Harbour Christian Fellowship's parking lot, which is covered by a heat-sagged green-and-white–striped tent. The adjacent church building is framed in white clapboards and carved into the edge of a small forest, pines and birches leaning in like pointed fingers. That carving is scratching deeper and deeper to make room for a newer, larger sanctuary that will, when finished, easily double the size of the current building.

The reason for the expansion is simple: we've grown too big for the current sanctuary. The church started just a few years ago; a small but passionate group of new Christians, mostly in their twenties and thirties, meeting on Sundays in the tiny library of Belknap College. My parents are among them, with their nine-year-old daughter, and sons aged three and one. When the numbers exceed the library's allotment of folding chairs, the core group—Pastor Gene, and other church leaders we refer to as elders—springs for the nearby white New Englander. There is barely any money, but what their wallets lack, their souls make up for in faith. *The Lord will provide*, they say, and will keep saying, as the numbers grow from a few dozen into a few hundred.

By the time I reach age six, there is no longer enough space in the building for Sunday School, no place to keep us occupied while Pastor Gene preaches sermons about how investing faith will bring huge yields—*ask and it shall be given unto you.* The elders decide it is time to build, and so each Sunday when it is time to pass around the tithing basket, further requests for money come through phrases such as "If the Lord has laid it upon your heart to donate to the new building fund, please consider doing so."

In the summer months prior to the building being finished, our Sunday School leader, Mrs. Holly, leads the congregation's children out to the parking lot where we sit under the big tent. There are so many children now that we've stopped calling it Sunday School, and instead say "Kid's Church." It is not a place for learning so much as it is designed for our own individual expressions of a budding faith. As a seven-year-old, I stare at the chair backs, puzzled by the odd acronyms messily spray-painted on the back: NCF, LCF, Adirondack Direct. It is in Kid's Church that I first meet Paul Howard, who will soon join me in second grade this fall at Laconia Christian School. On his first day visiting the church a few months ago, I had made fun of the faded, tight polo shirt pulled over his skinny frame, and after the service his mother approached me saying, "Be nice to Paul. He doesn't have any friends here." It seemed like a good idea, so I walked over to him, extended my hand, and said, "We're friends, ok?"

Now, we sit in the second row and wait for Mrs. Holly to pick up her dreadnaught acoustic guitar and lead us in songs that have lines like "If I was a fuzzy wuzzy bear/I'd thank you Lord for my fuzzy wuzzy hair."

In her floral dress, pinks and greens spilling over the guitar, she announces, "Today will be our last day in the kid's tent everyone!" Last year, we stayed under the spacious freedom of the tent until the end of the summer forced us back to the cramped upper rooms of the sanctuary, where faint sermons floated through the squeaky floorboards. But it is the middle of June, and I don't understand why the exodus is happening so soon.

"The new sanctuary is almost complete, and there's getting to be so many of you out here," she continues, informing us that next Sunday we'll meet in the old sanctuary while the adults break in the seats of the new building.

I've seen the new seats. They are a hideous, cushioned pink. Rather than fold, they interlock into rigid rows. I get the impression that the adults can't wait to claim their new spots. *Your sermons better be good Gene, or else we'll all fall asleep in those luxury seats!* The congregation wants to get comfortable, but I like shifting restlessly for two hours, not letting any part of me fall asleep.

"Before the first song, would any of you like to share?" Mrs. Holly says, as is typical at the beginning of the children's portion of the service. "I bet Joey does," I say to Paul out of the corner of my mouth. Every Sunday during Kid's Church Joey answers the invitation and marches to the front of the room, his sweaty, red-dotted face singing with an operatic smile.

"Oh—*Joey*—do you have a new song for us?" she asks, noticing his stubby arm sticking out of the mass of gray chairs and children. "Well, come on up!"

He always has a new song. He makes one up on the spot every time, the lyrics squeezing like water from a Nerf ball out of his brain, comprised of verses and scriptural paraphrases he'd picked up in church. He believes that melody is created by adding violent vibrato to every syllable of a word.

"Je-e-e-zuh-uh-uh-uhs / di-i-i-i-ed / o-o-on th-th-the / cr-cr-ah-ah-ss-ss . . ." he belts out with sincere conviction. I can't take it—I can never take it. Paul gives me one look and I lose it. I stretch the collar of my shirt over my mouth, biting my tongue, cheeks, lips, anything to keep the laughter from seeping through, and in so doing soak my collar with laugh drool, and even still, there is nothing to be done to contain the laughter.

The dirt floor under the tent is the same parking lot that I play freeze tag on with all the other church kids after Pastor Gene says "Amen" to the crowd before him at the end of each service. To my parents and the older parishioners, his word is a signal to lower the drawbridge connecting the sacred and secular. Inside the church they are saints, outside, they go back to being my friends' parents. But the worlds swirl in my head, and I can't determine what is church and what is play. When Joey sings, Mrs. Holly hears a young boy earnestly connecting to a Savior that died on the cross for his sins. To me, it seems he's merely parroting the kind of angelic lingo that brings the spotlight over his freckled face.

"Bryan and Paul," Mrs. Holly says, her eyes blazing through her thick pink glasses. "Please move to the *back* row." She doesn't know it, but she is part of the game, and just bumped us up to the next level. Paul and I move to the rear then crawl under the metal chairs, row by row, racing to see who can get back to our original seats first. Somehow, no one notices, and my head keeps swirling.

For the next few Sundays we meet in the old sanctuary as planned, Paul and I collar-soaking and chair-crawling as if nothing has changed. One Sunday, however, toward the end of Kid's Church, my mom comes in and taps my brother Caleb and me on the shoulders, and motions us out the door. "Are we going out to eat?" I whisper as I take her hand and a tambourine of metal bracelets jangles on her wrist. She doesn't answer, her eyes fixed intently on the exit.

Out in the parking lot, dozens of people move towards their cars. Elders Rick and Scott stop and gather a group of adults in a circle, while my brother Caleb and I walk around, poking our heads in to listen. The group joins hands as Rick prays aloud, "Lord, please give Gene guidance, and us guidance as we make our way through this very confusing situation. Let your will be done in the midst of this."

Without any further explanation, my family climbs into our blue Dodge Caravan and pulls out of the parking lot for the last time. I will never fully understand why the church splits. I try to make sense of the various rumors I gather over the next few weeks: something about the way money was handled, or something said/done that was considered blasphemous, maybe all of the above. Whatever it was, whole sections of the new pink chairs keep their chemical new scent.

Game 1: Pastor

Normally during lunch recess, my fellow fifth graders and I play two-hand touch football on the graveled parking lot at Laconia Christian School. But today, our curiosity has gotten the better of us. Paul and I lead a group into the woods that all but swallow the school grounds—"past the bounds," we reverently say—and make our way to an overgrown outdoor chapel. It feels almost mythical—a limbo of moldy holiness. We first found the chapel in third grade, and I had asked Paul to perform a wedding ceremony for Amber York and me. My classmates sat on the stone pews and watched as Amber stutter-stepped down the grassy aisle. Standing straight and cupping his pale hands like an open Bible, Paul prompted us and we said *I do*, then exchanged a pair of neon plastic rings I had won playing Skee-Ball.

Now in fifth grade, we gather in a similar fashion and play "pastor." I stand at a worm-tracked podium that is tilting but still standing, and I address this church of our own with a sermon based on what I've heard so far:

"Blah blah blah Moses. Blah Blah Blah *Mo*ses. Amen. Please help put away the chairs."

2

I clearly state to Mom that I want nothing to do with a new church. Mom says, "We're going." In an effort to stick together, members of the Centre Harbour diaspora pooled some money, made some calls, and began renting an old fire station in Weirs Beach on the weekends, soon to be called Cornerstone Christian Fellowship. "You'll get to see all your old friends," she reassures me. I know that Paul's family isn't going there, so I know she's lying.

We walk in to what must've been a break room or function hall for the firemen. I scan the hospital-tiled room: not a single kid my age. Towards the back I see Rick and Scott grabbing metal folding chairs off of large stacks in the back, and I exhale for the first time since walking in.

The desire to keep our once-thriving community from flat-lining has pushed Rick and Scott into being interim church leaders, in addition to their normal roles as worship leaders—those in charge of leading the congregation in song for the first part of the service. Rick plays a trebly twelve-string, Scott a deep six, and since neither of them sees himself as a preacher, the two-hour service often turns into an extended time of worship.

To fill awkward silences, I hear people speaking in tongues—a gift that our nondenomination believes is relevant in the modern church, unlike most mainline denominations like Baptists and Presbyterians who believe its use was restricted to the New Testament. The idea is that once God's Spirit has filled you, an otherworldly phrase wells up from your soul, jumps the spirit-body divide, and falls out of the mouth repeatedly. "Shuddah bineh hundai, O Lord" I hear over lightly picked chord progressions of D to D suspended. The Scriptures teach that a person should not publicly speak in tongues without someone who has the gift of interpretation. Though this fact is mentioned during sermons about speaking in tongues, in practice, I've yet to hear anyone step up and interpret.

The songs we sing now are slow and in minor keys. It seems everyone is still in a frozen state of shock. How could our community splinter at a time of such seeming prosperity? In an attempt to reclaim that old fire, Scott and Rick break into "Jehovah Jireh, My Provider," a "Hava Nagila"-style tune that used to send my mom and many others clapping and kicking into the aisles—a move we referred to as the charismatic two-step. I always knew it was coming when I looked down at her feet to see if she'd push off her heels. This time, she slides off one of her black flats, but only to reach down and rub a sore toe.

At the end of the service, my dad ushers us into our new forest green Caravan—dual sliding doors now—and I buckle myself into the stiff new seating, hoping that today will be one of the days when I can convince my parents to stop at Paugus Diner for a triple egg omelet.

"Oh, I forgot my Bible," says Mom. "Bryan, run in and grab it."

I am happy to be buckled in, securely removed from the fire station. I want to pull a *why me?* but I know that will kill any omelet hopes. I run back in, find the Bible, and turn to the door. Scott stops me before I get there: "The Lord has a special plan for you, you know." I nod a slow affirmative. He then puts a wide, callous-tipped left hand on my head and begins praying over me. The blood is pumping in my eardrums so loud I can't even understand what he is saying. I listen closer: it is in tongues.

"Hashum bah lililalie, yes Lord, yes Lord, ha shumbilicalcord, oh Lord."

He opens his eyes, pats my thick brown hair and says, "Remember that ok? That wasn't from me, that was from the Lord." I nod slowly again and walk in a daze back to the minivan.

"What took you so long?" my mother asks. With the same vacant look of surprise I've had since Scott started talking to me, I continue shaking my head slowly and buckle my seat belt.

Game 2: Tongues

Before bed, Tommy French is crawling around his living room floor looking for something for us to play with. It is Friday night, I am seven and Tommy is eight. I'd rather be sleeping over at Paul's house, but Tommy's mother had asked my mother if I could spend some time with her lonely, hyperactive son.

"Here it is!" he cries, holding up two halves of the arm cast he just had removed a week ago. "Do you want to wear it?" he says, not so much asking me as spewing formalities. He scrambles over on all fours to a desk, grabs a roll of masking tape and then moves towards my right arm. He clasps it around my forearm, a gasp and thud of air closing around it. As his mom and dad look on from their faded sofa, he pinches an end of the tape, affixes it to the cast, and begins wrapping it around like he is patching a roof.

I look up to his mom, hoping for something like, "Tommy, stop putting your friend in a cast," but when I start to say something to her, she cuts me off, saying, "Well, Tommy had to wear that for two months, I think you can handle it for one night."

Later, Tommy lays out the sleeping bags in the living room, and as his dad turns out the light, Tommy says, "Dad, can you speak in tongues before we go to sleep?"

"Well, sure," Mr. French says, acting like his son just asked for a glass of water. He bends over us, the smell of sawdust puffing out from his hunter-plaid button-up, his thick red mustache residing above us like a halo. "Rrrrah-bo-bo-bo," he begins, the hairs over his mouth trilling with the r's, spittle hitting my upper lip. I try to wipe it off with my right arm, before remembering that it's buried under four inches of tape and plaster. "Rah-rah-bo-bo-bo," he continues. Tommy squirms in delight like his favorite bedtime story has just reached its happy ending, and I feel trapped.

3

The first day we attend Laconia Christian Fellowship—the church affiliated with Laconia Christian School, meeting in its gymnasium—I'm almost run down by a congregant in a silk purple dress with long ribbons attached to her wrists and enough makeup on that I can imagine her applying it with a cheese spreader. When she lifts her arms toward me, I assume she's attempting to shake my hand in welcome, but her eyes stay vacant, and she passes me by, apparently far more interested in how the ribbons trail the movement of her arms.

In order to conveniently invoke a sense of holiness in the multipurpose gym, basketball hoops are decorated with streamers, while school spirit posters are shoddily covered with purple banners arranged with felt cutouts of letters, crowns, and/or lambs. The slogans emblazoned on these church spirit posters, when paired with the half-blocked volleyball and b-ball pin-ups behind them, read: "KING OF KINGS–Put It Thru For 2!!" and "Spike It Down Their Throats–LAMB OF GOD."

As my family and I step out of the foyer into the gymnasium, we walk slowly, turning our heads constantly in hopes that we'll see someone we know. Even though everyone is still standing around, the worship band has started leading the congregation in song, leaving us to rush to the nearest row with five open seats. I'm relieved to see that grey folding chairs with odd acronyms painted on the back rest below the congregation, some even look like they were pilfered from Centre Harbour's old sanctuary.

After repeating the chorus of "Sing a Song of Celebration" for about three-and-a-half minutes, the song ends and the worship leader invites all the children to the front of the room for the next song. Mom looks at me; I mouth "*no way*" and grab my cold chair with my hands. She looks at Caleb, and being that he is a sociable ten to my awkward twelve, he sidesteps through the aisle and joins the mass of kids up front. The worship team strums into a song called "Bring Forth the Royal Robe." I figure that this is what the purple woman had been attempting when she led her ribbon processional almost into my face. As if they are a coin-operated teacup ride, all the kids form a circle, join hands and start walking around and around. My mom looks relieved that at least one of her sons questioned her judgment.

The children look incredibly serious, as if this was a warm-up to a ritualistic cleansing: "Yes, now that we have all marched in a circle seven times clockwise and seven times counterclockwise, let us bring forth the anointing oil," they seem to suggest. I'm not far off—during prayer time, a church official runs into the office off the sanctuary and reemerges with a plastic vial of oil—vegetable? Olive? They lay hands on a woman who's recently been through a divorce, and dab her head with oil. I picture a fingerprint of zits forming on her forehead. The only thing keeping me from running and hiding in the minivan is the familiarity of the folding chair. The chair is sitting on the foul line—the spot where, two days prior, I scored ten points in a JV boy's basketball game. I am praying where I was just playing.

After an hour-long sermon that made use of incomprehensible words such as *hermeneutics* and *Shekinah glory*, Pastor Chris says "Amen." The congregation bends at the knees slightly and simultaneously reaches down to pick up their coats like a father leaning for his wallet at a restaurant. "Before you leave," Pastor Chris continues, "could everyone lend a hand folding the chairs and putting them back in the closet?" More familiarity—I love this part. Putting away the chairs has become liturgical to me; I wait for this moment the way most everyone else waits for Communion. At this point, a priest swinging incense would be weird; folding as many chairs as I can carry is a holy offering.

Game 3: Hyssop

I am *it*. I hold a sopping, softball-shaped Nerf ball that I have just lifted out of the clear blue water of the in-ground pool in my backyard. The game is a hydro-soaked version of tag where the ball is thrown in hopes of hitting someone and making them *it*, as the players chaotically circle the water and the cement border that wraps around the peanut-shaped pool. Paul is running towards the diving board, his wet footprints trailing him along the stippled concrete. I prepare to invoke ritual.

In the New Testament account of Christ's crucifixion, it is said that while he is hanging on the cross, Jesus says that he is thirsty. Those who are mourning at his feet beg and plead the guards around him to offer some kind of meager comfort. A centurion sticks a sponge onto the end of a hyssop branch and dips it in a bitter wine. He then lifts the sponge and allows Jesus to quench his thirst. As a fourth-grader, this scene is just another image that is circulating in the dampness of my soft-wired brain, and it falls out as we make up rules for our version of this game of chase; this game where we are pursued and then forced to pursue before we even know what hits us. Our first reaction: get rid of what's been passed on to us.

I hold the dripping ball high aloft my head, like I am a reverend performing the sacrament of Communion. I speak the incantation in a deep, enunciated tone, "I drink of the Hyssop!" and then squeeze the bitter chlorine all over my face, the chemical water blending with the salt caking in my eyebrows. I open my eyes too early, and through the stinging blur, I can't quite make out the people and objects ahead of me. Nearly blind, I walk towards the pool in faith, hoping that it will be enough to keep me from falling over the edge.

[**Static** *is listening to the sonic dots, trying to touch the hem of the cosmic garment, to move from one place to another and not leave your problems to chase after you. In your father's death, you are trying to create a history from loud but invisible sparks, to add flesh to the outline of ghosts, to undo the sleeping separation between death and eternity, in hopes that you are not just another vibrating speck of fuzz.*]

4

Shape of a Ghost

Our house has become a series of mouths that digest our voices and sometimes burp up the acid reminder of what we once sounded like. The emanating sounds are most often the heartburned prayers of my family and my church, asking for a miracle for my father. Often the request turns into a bold present tense, some even going as far as thanking God for the miracle he's about to do—*thank you for taking away this burden, thank you for hearing us.* It is the spring of 1987, I am four, and that miracle has gotten steeper and steeper, until one day it is a cliff face, rain-slicked rocks slipping down, nothing even trying to go up. The closest thing to a miracle is that the hospital has honored my father's request to be at home when it happens.

When my mother pulls our rumbling white Bronco into the driveway in front of our unattached garage, my sister gets out without being asked and wrenches the garage door upward, its jaws cracking as it prepares to swallow the chalky pill. For the last time, my father gets out of a car and climbs the set of stairs leading up to our lemon-yellow house, my mother guiding him on one side, a rolling intravenous stand on the other. She peels the screen door open, pinning it with her hip as she pushes open the front door, letting all of us in. He waits as my mother strips the cushions off the woolen, brown sleeper sofa in the living room and rips out the tongue of springs and mattress coiled inside. When the sheets are taut and pillows propped, she guides him over and lays him down, checking the connections and levels on the IV stand, its tubes like rogue veins escaping the rot growing in the middle of his body. With tape and a square of gauze she secures a feeding tube three times the size of a drinking straw that is cinched to the side of his neck. It is not that he can't open his mouth and receive food, but that three-quarters of his stomach is gone. She is a registered nurse and so she is quick, thorough, letting habit hide the fact that she's placing her husband on his deathbed.

The couch is ancient and noisy, though the body on top of it barely rustles its springs and rusting supports. He's always on the left edge of the bed, the leash of his feeding tube not giving him much slack, but it makes him easier to reach. His head is propped up so that he is facing the door, watching us enter and leave at whim, effortlessly performing what he now must think of as a miraculous action.

Because he can barely move, he becomes an object, human furniture. Or, maybe furniture becomes him, maybe nothing is inanimate if we notice that everything has the power to ingest a soul, swallow its ghost. That couch becomes the fuzzy lips between life and death. Each passing day he is more a part of the house as his body moves closer to the inanimate, his skin dying before he does, invisibly flaking off and sinking into sheet and mattress. My father is a couch, the couch an urn.

I am trying to figure out the quickest way to get to his side of the couch as I walk in from the dining room. I take stuttered paces in both directions, behind, in front, over, nothing feeling quite right. My mother is sitting with him, holding a mug of hot broth in one hand. They're talking, but the words disappear before I can register their tones, let alone the shape of the words themselves. The room glows with silence. With her free hand, my mother pushes her brown hair over her ear, but most of it falls back into her face. She picks up what looks like a long lollipop stick with a small green sponge stuck to the end and dips it into the broth. She lifts it out, moves her hand up and down as if she is trying to guess the weight of the object, letting a few drops fall back into the steaming murk. My father opens his mouth: I get a little bit closer, still not sure if the route I've chosen is the way to get the nearest to him. It is during these feeding times that I can see his mouth the clearest, can see how the act of eating and breathing, letting things in and out is tiring for him, his front-heavy glasses tipping slightly over the slope of his nose. He is not speaking here—and yet I imagine would-be words slipping into the broth. My mother rests the foam square on his cracking tongue and presses lightly to make sure the salty liquid comes out and moisturizes it. His head cranes upward, guiding the broth down into a dark, wordless throat.

Even though I'm trying to stop it, I can feel this day—like every day since he came home—turning into a silent slide, a static projection of where my father is and what he is doing. Or, rather, what he is not doing because that's all he can do. The lenses of my eyes are trying to capture him, record his every last move, but I blink and he stays put; I blink again and I've looked away from the couch, staring at a clay coin bank in the shape of a duck. Its beak is closed, but is chipping off at the top, carving out a new, awkward mouth. I pick it up from it's corner on the floor, lifting its head back, and then feel how the pounds of pennies heavy in its stomach make it sink like a footprint back into the thick, green carpet. Even though it is broken, we keep it here in a corner by the doorway into the dining room. Through the crack in the brittle beak a thin metal rod is exposed, an iron bone that keeps its mouth shut while we feed it our extra, unnecessary change, expecting it all back when we decide it amounts to something again, and we drain its worth.

I feel overexposed. If my eyes are a camera, then the camera cannot take in all the images that populate my house, all the bright things that surround the dim object of my father. I continue to circle and haunt the couch; then I'm standing by him as my mother continues dipping and feeding. Somehow I've already forgotten how I got here. I look back at where I started, hoping there will be a row of indentations tracking what I did so that I can remember it later when I want to return.

I want to pick up his thinning wrist, to see if the blanket below carries the impression of his arm, or if it is so light that there is no crease at all, the blanket already numb to the memory of a body part resting on it. I run a finger over the lattice-ridged strip of medical tape that secures the feeding tube in his neck, the tape's crisp plasticity a reminder that it is not skin, that I am not touching my father. It looks as if we are sticking him back together as the cracks in his person deepen, lengthen, until our patch-up job is an empty spool of tape, a pinched bag of saline with a tube no longer connected to a body.

As for houses, my family has had three all together, although that togetherness splits with each move. First, we live in half a house on Jefferson Street, where my little brother Caleb will be brought after he is born. Here, Caleb and I are bathed in a kitchen sink, warmed by a potbellied stove, and put to bed in the same room as my older sister Allyson. One night on

Jefferson Street I have a dream that I am flying down the stairs, moving so slowly it is as if I am haunting, not flying, my body parallel to the decline of the stairs. My shadow slinks below me, it staggers like an accordion as it slips over the lip of each step. I am aware that my father is walking around, though even in the dream I can't find evidence of his movements, the timbre of words blown beneath his mustache. The dream becomes a tripped loop: I keep getting halfway down the stairs, just to the point where maybe my parents are talking in the kitchen, but as I approach I am suddenly starting over at the top of the stairs again, rounding the corner from my bedroom. I do not know if there is an end to the dream, nor if the loop is meant to go nowhere forever.

We move down the block to Elm Street in 1986, and it is meant to be temporary; just a next step towards the house my parents envision for their family's future. Though he has gotten sick by this point, we think he'll beat it, that God will provide like we always say he does. So, when they put a down payment on the Elm Street house, having the master bedroom up a flight of stairs doesn't seem like a bad idea to my dad, that reaching that height might only be possible for a fraction of the short time he will live here. And though they are making payments to own this house, it is not ours in the way my parents want. They want to build, to shape something of their own that begins with them and, maybe, never ends—it'll be a space where every couch, chair, crumpled receipt, tracked-in dirt speck will carry our story, our heritage. When one of us sits on that future chair, it'll be an extension of our bodies, our eyelashes and lint fusing into a symbiosis of sparkling biology and inanimation, separated by nothing but our buried shadows.

Not long after we move to Elm Street my parents take a leap of faith and buy land up on Meredith Center Road—literally just down the street from a Christian school that is barely older than my nine-year-old sister, where they are hoping to save enough money for all three of us to attend.

It is as if from puberty to thirty, Jesus slept, and all that time in between is some endless dream. There is no record of him growing armpit hair, of him wondering what life would've been like if he hadn't grown up with a stepfather, of his roaring twenties when he learned to live without "a place to lay his head." His childhood is a spectral etching in which we can imagine he could've asked about his origins, his heritage, his identity. The writers of the

Gospels seem to wonder the same thing. Matthew opens his version with a genealogy that traces Jesus back to Abraham and the creation of Israel. Luke places his genealogy—this one going all the way back to Adam—in between the only canonical story of Jesus' youth and when he is baptized at age thirty.

In this one account, Jesus is twelve, and has traveled with a large group of family and friends to Jerusalem for Passover. When they leave, Jesus stays behind, and the parents of the Messiah don't notice his absence for a whole day. They turn back and eventually find him in the temple courts, theologizing with priests. When they tell him that they've been anxiously looking for him, he asks, "Why were you searching for me?" Here, a set of parents is looking for a son, who at this point is just that, a son, not Son, and so Jesus sounds ignorant of the fact that parents would rather not lose sight of their children. But then, all searching has to stem from a loss, from walking away from the thing we valued most, assuming it would follow us wherever, whenever, and then we kill ourselves trying to figure out why we can't hear that voice anymore, can't even see a shifting shadow or a fading impression. So we scour frantically, even if all we find are the shiny spots on the floor where the furniture of the past once stood. Before it was moved, before it was sold, before it was left on the curb for a week, and someone drives by, thinks about picking it up, but then, *it rained yesterday*, so she keeps driving.

Before his father can answer his first question, he follows up with another, and then, *duh*, it's so obvious: "Didn't you know I had to be in my father's house?"

The night my father dies, I am not in his house. My mom's mother, who we all call Nanny, is babysitting me, and in a rare case, Caleb is not with me. Though he is two years younger than me, we're often grouped together like twins, or one person even, in light of the fact that my sister is so much older. For six years, it was just Mom, Dad, and Allyson. As my father's time runs out, my mother needs more and more time—with him, with making *preparations*. The kids, then, are being watched by a number of sitters, but seldom are the three of us under the same roof. Caleb and I are at the Tuckers' or Nanny's, and Allyson is at the Chisholms'. We are listed as *Bryan, Caleb, and Allyson, the boys and Allyson* or, more often, *Allyson and the boys*; that *and* always separating us, a divided house, houses dividing us.

41

In the late afternoon of May 14, Nanny is unpacking a bag I have with me, and I realize that I will not be sleeping at home tonight. I do not know where my siblings are, nor do I know the reason why my mother won't be picking me up in a few hours, or if there is something that is keeping her from doing it.

The inside of Nanny's house is always dark, so the sun surprises me when a breeze briefly parts a curtain and cuts a slice of light onto the cherry-stained wood paneling, day breathing in, night breathing out, the exhalation always lasting longer than the pulling in. I can't sit still, and for some reason I keep running between her one bedroom and the living room around the corner. I bend myself endlessly over that division between bed and living, stopping abruptly in the middle of each room and turning about-face as if I had hit a wall that wasn't there, or I was tied to a giant elastic, and there is only so far I can go before I'm snapped back. When I first arrived, Nanny let me open an amber glass candy dish in the living room and pick out a butterscotch or a peppermint. I wait until she isn't looking, answering yet another phone call that causes her to turn and hunch away from me, and as she folds her neck down into the receiver and speaks in a zipped whisper, I try lifting the half-shell cover without *ting*ing the glass edge too loudly, or crinkling the dead-skin wrapper that shrouds the candy.

When we turn in for the night, she lies on one side of the bed, I lie on the other, the sugar still buzzing my thoughts into a speeding, itching blur. I squirm under the prickly quilt, pushing my body up and down, trying in vain to press my weight deeper into a mattress that feels like a plank of wood with an old sheet wrapped tightly around it. Nanny is either asleep or she understands the discomfort and doesn't tell me to stop my fussing. When sleep comes, it is as surprising as that thin burst of sun, and so when the phone rings the next morning and my eyes shoot open, I can't really believe that I've ever actually been asleep. Nanny's tone is hushed, but she can only lean her body so far away from me in this full size bed, so the mutterings are louder, more frantic than what she thinks she sounds like. But then there is a gasp that breaks her tone completely and she is covering her mouth, shaking, and I get up, start running around the edge of the bed, then out around the corner into her, not my, not my father's, living room, and I stop completely when I hit the uninterrupted blackness.

In the Gospel of Luke Jesus says, "the Son of Man has no place to lay his head," no space dedicated for rest. I am the son of a man, not capitalized, of a man with no place to lay a headstone. I do have a place to lay my head, but big deal, right? What is sleep but the amount of time we put aside to forget? Sleep is a drug that none of us ever recovers from—our eyelids get heavier until one day they are not like morning-drawn curtains but doors to a bank vault, and then it's that thing people call eternal sleep.

But, we also dream, and Hamlet, the ghost-talker, said that was the rub. Before we wake, rubbing crust from our eyes, dreams try to remind us of the things we were sleeping to forget. The waifish images haunt our rest; lies that walk around and have mouths that tell us we can fly and gather ashes, taking back what should've been ours.

My father has no headstone, no plot where a rock sticks up jagged as if the grassy gums of the earth are cutting crooked, marbled teeth. He wanted his ashes spread over the property he and my mother had purchased and planned to pour a concrete foundation on, and from there, encourage growth. He bought the land before he ever knew that esophageal cancer was the reason he had to pop Rolaids so often—over twenty-five acres for $17,000. With a chainsaw my mother had given him for Christmas, he set about clearing the land himself, having a gravel driveway laid down over the eighth-of-a-mile stretch snaking up to the plot. When he'd carved a chunk out of the darkened forest's stomach, my mother started packing picnics and bringing us all up to play house on our land. After finishing her sandwich one afternoon, she walked over the land and climbed up a tree on the periphery, and with one hand hooked around the trunk like a banister, she waved, yelling to her children, her husband, "This is the view from the second floor! From our master bedroom!"

When he dies, my mother sells the property, knowing this jilted square of earth is just a myth. But not quite a myth, as that suggests a past, memories built on top of each other like posts and beams, clapboarding their way to myth, legacy. No, this is a stunted myth, peppered with the burnt fragments of a future. Her one condition to the owners is that every year on May 15th, she be allowed to drive up the soon-to-be-paved driveway and walk the edge of the land, praying, crying, and singing out of tune, her shoes sinking into the soft earth as if she were trying to plant him, to keep him from blowing away farther.

Since it was sold, I visit this would've-been spot once, but it is only by chance. Three years after my mother is remarried to a man named James, I am in fourth grade at Laconia Christian School, but I am playing basketball for a city league team named St. James. When my father was alive, my parents wracked their brains with ideas on how they might pay my tuition. It never occurred to them that, because of the life insurance policies in my father's name, it would never be a financial burden.

Jared Hutchinson is on St. James, too, his cowlicked black hair framing the enormous Rec-Specs he wears during games. My position is the center, since I am the tallest kid in the room. "Hey Parish! Parish! Pass the ball!" my teammates yell during practice, modifying my last name to fit with Robert Parish, the 7'1" center for the Boston Celtics. In the middle of the season, Jared announces that he'll be hosting a team sleepover at his house. They are all public school kids, so they are all strangers to me. My mother convinces me that it would be good if I went, and, she says, did you know he lives on the property that was almost ours?

When our van pulls up the driveway, I am only vaguely aware that, amongst the crab grass and rotting piles of leaves, my father's ashes surround me. This knowledge, mixed with the anxiety I feel about having to talk to these other kids, keeps me silent. There is pizza, cake, a plastic indoor basketball hoop. The talking around me doesn't stop, but is never directed at me. Alex Conniston won't shut up. I want to yell, *Everyone out of my house*, but instead I pick a corner of the living room and wait for someone to remember to pass the ball to me. Lucas Paley finally sees me, yells, "Heads up, Parish!" Here, on the land of my father, no one has any idea who I am, and they won't call me by my real name.

That night we cover the cold living room floor with our sleeping bags, and I have trouble finding a space for mine, carrying it around like a snapped chrysalis. I try to step around Alex, who hasn't stopped talking, and my heel rolls over his blanketed foot. "What the hell, Parish?" he says, before going back to rambling. There is a small space around the corner of the couch, so I lay my sleeping bag down, wrapping it around splayed torsos. I crawl in, shivering, and press my head against the fabric of the couch leg, and though it feels unnatural, as if it doesn't fit, I don't move. I am freezing and wide awake, listening as a few snores begin, Alex still talking to no one, *shut up Alex*, me not sleeping, me conjuring cartoon shapes of ghosts outside the window.

For thirty years, Jesus didn't ask anyone to follow him, or ask them to leave their houses behind and wander the known world trying to find someone, anyone, that would recognize who he was. He didn't tell anyone about his true parentage, about the fact that even though he was raised in a good home, it never felt truly his own, never something he could inhabit for very long. *Who does he think he is*, his disciple Simon might've thought, *the Messiah?* Instead he waited, kept wandering, doing, never speaking, and then in Matthew 16:15, he asks Simon, "But who do you say that I am?" Simon says, "You are the Messiah." And, instead of breathing a huge sigh of relief and thinking *Phew! I was beginning to think I was alone on this one*, he changes Simon's name to Peter, which means "the rock," saying that the church, his house, will be built on this rock. But then he tells Peter to keep his declaration a secret. What Simon says, Simon believed, and then his heritage was reset, swallowed.

Part Two: **Night / Light**

[**Night** *is a descent—like a curtain, a mouth closing, a quilt pulled across eyes that won't close. But you are told,* heaven is above, hell is below, *and there you are in the middle, swearing as day dies out that the ground seems hot under your heels, and if you could just be good enough you might keep it below you, keep it from coming up in conversation, in dreams. As your pillowed eyes look for sleep, the darkness thickens, arises, because it only comes out at night. Descending, ascending—it doesn't matter where it comes from, only what the last six letters of both words spell out.*]

5

Thief in the Night

In third grade at Laconia Christian, Mrs. Franklin tells us, "In heaven, you'll all be given new names." Sitting next to me, Paul immediately crouches over his faux-wood desk and starts scribbling ideas, a triangular smile rising up to meet the pale freckles dotting his cheekbone.

"I like Jase," he whispers to me, looking down at his list with pride. "No, wait—Jaws!"

"Those are both from movies," I tell him, pulling the collar of my striped polo shirt over my mouth, as has become our main method to help muffle the sound. "What makes you think God will let you have a name from *Ice Pirates*?" I'm fairly upset about this prospect. In kindergarten, it took me a lot of one-on-one time with Mrs. Orr in order to get the Ys right in my first and last name. They dip down below the blue line in my notebooks, getting in everyone else's way, demanding to be noticed. "I kind of just want to keep mine."

"That's no fun! Don't you get it? You have the chance to be completely different." Since his parents divorced when he was in first grade, his dad rarely acknowledges his sister's and his existence. I imagine this is why he wears his given name like a too-tight turtleneck.

"Yeah, but what if you don't like the new one?"

"And," Mrs. Franklin continues, slightly louder, her eyes jumping towards us as they follow the *aaaa* sound from her mouth, "the streets will be paved with gold, and we'll become angels, singing before the throne of God for all eternity!"

"Gosh, does anything sound more boring?" I mutter to Paul.

"I think it sounds awesome."

"But how will I find you if you're floating in some big group of see-through singers and answering only to Jaws? And," I continue, getting increasingly louder and more upset, "how am I supposed to find my dad in all that?"

Paul doesn't answer. I inadvertently said *dad*—a word that, for both of us, no longer connects to the physical world in the way it used to. Among the only comforts I have been able to take from my father's death four years ago are the words that seem to come from everyone's lips, even if they aren't Christians.

"You know, Buggy, you'll see him again in heaven," my aunt Linda had told me outside my front door as we got ready for the funeral in May of 1987. I stared back at her, my four-year-old brain spinning like a warped bike tire around the words: *death, forever, heaven, eternity*. Her face cracked at the corners of her eyes as she waited for a response she knew there was no way I could form, and long, wet stripes of mascara tracked down her face as if she were a painting that someone was trying to restore—black paint filling fissures carved by the blade of time. I did not see her turn away, but suddenly became aware of the screen door swinging with an arthritic whine, the back of her black dress flapping from the movement, her hands grasping the sides of her head.

"I just hope it's not a boring name like 'Michael' or something," Paul concedes.

"Paul! Bryan!" Mrs. Franklin yells out. "That's it! You're both staying in at lunch recess with your heads down at your desk."

"Ugh," says Paul. "That'll be like an eternity!"

That night I have a recurring dream that has been buzzing around my head like a deerfly. I am at an unfamiliar church that is completely round and situated at the top of a hill. I am trying to get to Sunday School, but no matter how many times I walk around the hallway, the right door never shows up. Instead, each door either has a picture of Jesus or Satan. The faces are colored bas-reliefs—the picture of Christ is blue and white, with the brown hair and shining, Renaissance countenance found in most Christian education textbooks. I want to ask the face of Jesus if my dad is in there, and if I can see him, but I can't get the words out. As is expected, Satan's picture is red and black. The fear I have of the door is not the one I'm accustomed to. It is more like a fixated puzzlement. My mouth bends and forms the question, "What are *you* doing here?"

"The end is nigh, my people," a visiting speaker at church tells us one Sunday at Laconia Christian Fellowship when I am in middle school. The man has been introduced to us as a prophet—someone Pastor Chris had met at one pastors' conference or another, where, as he said, "All sorts of powerful moves of God are happening." This is not the first time a prophet has visited, and the message always starts the same way: "The Day of the Lord is fast approaching, brethren. Are you ready?"

Everyone in the congregation is beaming with excitement at the prospect of something miraculous happening in our cold New England church. I am not beaming. In fact, from what I've read of prophets in the Old Testament, my reaction seems to be more in context: I am scared to death.

There are only two topics in church that move me beyond boredom and into desperate terror: prophecies and apocalyptic sermons. And when a prophet is in town, he generally comes bearing some warning that our time is almost up.

So on prophet Sundays, I have to pee a lot.

Frequent trips to the bathroom can't allow me to completely avoid the lengthy sermons on the final judgment of the earth. At twelve years old, I am too young to understand the terms—like *post-millenialist, amillennialist, pre-tribulation, post-trib, mid-trib*—that represent the countless interpretations of St. John's dreams in Revelation, the final book of the New Testament. I do understand when they use the words *plagues, eternal suffering, mark of the beast,* and *left behind.*

Despite the predicted bleak state the world would be in after Christ's return, these sermons seemed to make everyone around me ecstatic. They have a blessed assurance that they'll be taken to heaven before the apocalyptic melee, so the more dramatic the post-rapture world is, the more heavenly anticipation they experience.

And today is no different. The prophet is fired up about hellfire.

In those days, brothers and sisters, there will be great famine and pestilence. Families will turn against each other, and a leader will arise from the confusion and will promise peace. But he will not bring peace. He will be the antichrist, and his main objective will be to bring violence. And to kill anyone who claims allegiance to God! That is why, brothers and sisters, your hearts must be prepared now.

I want to prepare my heart so I can avoid this, but I'm not sure how to do so. I wait for the prophet to offer some how-tos.

In the middle of a sentence, as if the glass of water he's been sipping is colder than he anticipates, the prophet winces tightly and grabs the upper corner of his forehead. "Is there someone here that suffers from chronic stomach pain?"

Much to my disbelief, there is.

Like an orangutan that has been let out if its cage, the prophet abandons his post at the front of the gymnasium-turned-sanctuary and rushes among us, teaching and praying over all those he could see were afflicted. I am frozen in my folding chair, trying to put all fears of what he's been talking about out of my head. I'm scared I could be transmitting these thoughts to his borderless mind, thus causing him to see a brown-haired boy who likes his name and doesn't want the world to end.

On a day when we would normally take out our seventh-grade history books, our teacher, Mrs. Carey says, "Ok; let's push the desks back and arrange the chairs in a semicircle up front," situating us for a movie. Metal legs are pulled over the thin brown carpeting in our classroom, the innards of the rickety desks spilling out and dragged underneath the desk's feet. One of my favorite pens is among the fallen, crushed by the metal, and its black ink slips down the handle. I lurch to grab it before it can stain the floor, and it smears into my palms. Staring at it as if it is some kind of malevolent stigmata, I figure this gives me the option to excuse myself from part of the film, whose opening credits have started to roll.

The movie is *Image of the Beast*, part three of a four-film series depicting what it could be like to be left behind after Jesus comes back and takes his followers to heaven. Created over ten years from 1972 to 1982, a time when thousands of converted hippies—whose systems were not completely purged of LSD and Jefferson Starship—were convinced that the second coming of Christ would happen literally any day. A certain number of these converts even left their homes, jobs, and families to move to remote cabins on a hill somewhere and await heaven's taxi with fellow believers. Money wasn't a concern—who would need it in a place where municipal sidewalks were made of gold?

But while some of them selfishly moved away from society, many others set about the sensational task of convincing all nonbelievers around them that things were about to get really bad. So, with a limited budget, Russell Doughten, Jr.—who had gained industry credibility from working on the cult classic *The Blob*—created the *Thief in the Night* series to visually postulate just how awful things would soon get.

Shot in typical 1970s Technicolor—a style that frightened me even in *Pete's Dragon*—the movies follow a series of left-behinders as they struggle to survive the post-apocalyptic murderfest. The director goes to great lengths to show how unexpected the return was: unattended wooden spoons left in boiling pots, an electric razor buzzing on the edge of a manila-toned sink, crashed cars still running with perfectly folded outfits left on the seats—the fact that they are folded being somehow creepier than the clothes being left to fall crumpled to the floor.

Due to the terrible tape quality, the soundtrack warbles and dips violently in and out of tune, an unintentional added layer of fear plucking at my nervous gutstrings. When I later watch *Monty Python and the Holy Grail* at Paul's house I discover that it is the same score, and it ruins the movie's comedy for me forever.

Normally, watching a movie instead of hearing a lecture on European history is a longed-for treat. But since our screening of part one earlier this year, I have begun making my way to the back of the classroom whenever Mrs. Carey starts wheeling the creaky old tube TV out of the closet and up to the front of the room. With a notebook in hand, I try my hardest to ignore scenes that depict characters being arrested by the movie's soulless world police—the United Nations Imperium for Total Emergency (UNITE)—for not accepting an electronic microchip in either their wrist or forehead, that is used by all to take part in world commerce. The class knew to recognize this as the mark of the beast, and those who took it as people unwittingly pledging irrevocable allegiance to Satan.

Not wanting to use my excuse to leave the classroom at the beginning, I let the ink pool into the railroad track creases of my hand, cupping it and hoping no one will notice. The first scene picks up where the previous installment, *A Distant Thunder*, left off—with a captured woman who is told that she must either take the mark, or be put to death. I can tell she is contemplating saving her own life, but the decision renders her inert for too long. They strap her, face up, into a guillotine.

The ink in my hand starts to run as I stare at the woman's face, the camera rotating between her screams and her view of the dangling blade. Before the men from UNITE can release it however, an earthquake rushes in, sending them running. I think that God has spared her, until the shaking trips the guillotine, sending it screeching down from a POV angle and ending the woman's cries.

I lean over to Paul, whose eyes are feasting on the footage, his triangular grin firmly in place.

"Sheesh. That seems pretty barbaric."

"Yeah," he says, not even blinking. "It's amazing."

"It's worse than the Reign of Terror," I say, referencing the chapter on the French Revolution that we have been studying in Mrs. Carey's history class.

"Maybe, but these people deserved it."

"I don't know. It scares me like crazy. I keep freaking out in my head— what if I get left behind?"

"Well, these movies make me happy because I know I won't be around for the bad stuff. If you're afraid, then maybe you're not really saved."

This is when I stand up to escape. I show Mrs. Carey the blackness on my hand and wordlessly walk out of the darkened room. I run the faucet on full blast, letting the water stay on even after the ink fades into the tiny canals, tingeing my palm the dead color of ash. Looking for anything that will stop the blade of the guillotine from falling, over and over, through my frontal lobe, I pick up a salmon-tinted bottle of soap and sniff out its floral antiseptic. A bird makes a noise outside the window. I don't know what kind it is, but it is not a crow. I try to use every one of my senses at once. Soap, water, bird—I force the sensations into some kind of quaking choir that will carve the hell from my skull.

It doesn't work.

Going to bed has become an activity that I carry out slowly, trying to stave off the quiet knives of night as long as possible. I triple the amount of time spent brushing my teeth, diligently swishing the burning mint of fluoride rinse for the recommended minute, stretching it to two if my tongue can take it.

When there is nothing left to distract me, I walk into my room and unfold the squeaky frame out of my sofa bed's woolen cave, and then turn off the ceiling lamp. When I was given my own room a year ago, the old brown couch was already up here, in what had previously been the family room. The couch used to reside downstairs, where, for a few months, it had become my father's deathbed. Years later, when I was about to move in to the room and was asked if I wanted to keep the pullout or get my own twin bed, I felt I had no choice. I kept what to me had become a relic that, no matter how coffin-like, offered me a connection with my father.

With visions of abandoned spoons in simmering pots, I start to move. The pullout bed convulses as if someone is grabbing its legs and shaking it from side to side. I am convinced it is Satan. He taunts me—letting me know that it is he, not God, who is waiting for me. As a brown and yellow afghan shuffles against my unnerved spirit, I try to tell myself that I am creating the terror, that I have already accepted Christ as my savior during a youth group meeting in fifth grade. Or was it in a Christian education class in first grade? I know for sure that I was baptized at age ten because it was my idea. Surely that was enough to keep me out of the devil's vibrating clutches.

It is in this moment that I realize why churches send the youth to Sunday School during sermons. The grim themes of hell and the apocalypse are too much for their infant souls to handle. But since my church identifies itself as nondenominational—defining itself in terms of what it is not—we don't have the kind of budgets that national churches like Catholics and Methodists do. We often don't have enough money for supplies, the personnel to organize it, and sometimes, not even enough youth to justify a class. So the preached judgment swishes together with images of guillotines and microchips, and leaks into my dreams.

With the help of these video sessions, my nightmares from elementary school have returned. For the last week, they have started with the circular hilltop church. Soon, the scene melts and morphs into a dirt-brown saloon with orange flame lighting. Through peripheral vision, I see gruff, slicked patrons in tan leather coats and cabby hats, sidling, smoking, and smiling. I know there is a door to a basement somewhere and that if I see it, I should avoid it. But when I see it, I go through it. The steps lead into charcoal caves filled with stalagmites and stalactites. There are little caves all around me, and I know that if I see one with a red light shining out of it, I shouldn't go near it. When I see the red light, I go near it and look in. A burning Satan is confronting a dirty-blonde-haired woman. He lays her down, rolls her stomach open like a sardine can and eats the contents through a big grin he aims my way.

Tonight, I have put a Bible under my pillow. I rest one hand on it as I lie awake and watch passing cars light my window. I soon notice that the faint streetlights are casting a man-shaped shadow through my NBA-themed curtains. I know no one is actually there—making it prime fodder for a future dream—so I try not to give the man much thought.

In the sleep that follows this discovery, the man in the curtain speaks to me and tells me his name is Mr. Matches. His arms are always at his sides, and the silhouette of his head gazes at the far wall of my room, even when he is talking to me. He tells me that the shadow cast by the small bookshelf I'd made in Boy Scouts is a miniature buffalo he keeps as a pet and has named Buffeth. Having an apparent penchant for the naming of things, he moves on to my three pillows, referring to them one by one as Softee, Thinnee, and Carolous Linnaeus.

Look what happens when you flip the M in my name, he says. *"Matches" becomes "Watches."*

He does not appear in my dreams again, but in the following nights when Mr. Matches is formed out of the darkness, I confide in him.

"Hey, Mr. Matches. Could you smell the beef stroganoff mom made tonight? It was sick. I didn't think I'd ever get through it." From the mundane, I move on to the things that have tripped my fears like a trap door. "I just don't understand why they used a guillotine to kill off those who wouldn't take the mark. And why did they make the accused lie face up during the execution? Even Robespierre wasn't that cruel." His gaze remains fixed like a royal guard, and he doesn't answer when I ask if God sent him. Still, his silence seems holy and determined; the way Christ was when the angry mob shouted for his death sentence.

I keep talking, until my voice slows and my thoughts become less coherent. In this way, I am able to fall asleep.

In the shower the next morning, I rub the front of my neck, imagining the snap of a guillotine overhead. I scrub it with a pink washcloth until it feels raw, but still bisected. It feels like a choice. I lie down on the grime-stained floor of the tub, and push my cheek against one of the faint flower-shaped slip pads that have worn down so much they are no longer visible. I slowly close my eyes and the tepid stream disappears from vision.

When I spring my eyes back open, it feels like an awakening, and I am not sure how much time has passed. The water looks the same, and I assume it's only been a couple seconds, but the feeling is one of eternity. I do not know if my mom is still downstairs reading *Guidepost* at the dinner table, or if my dad is checking the scores from last night's Celtics game, or if my brother Caleb is pouring the milk for his Crispix. I do not know if the world I have woken up in is pre- or post-rapture. If I am left behind, I will not know until I finish my shower and run downstairs. I close, then reopen my eyes for a second time, and again I do not know where I have woken up.

[**Light** *swims and sinks into histories—the kinds you read about and the kinds you make up for yourself. Time travel is only possible when you are willing to admit that your life is a blinding flash that spins back beyond your own blood and into the shedding of blood. A bloodline is not just what connects you to a singular people—ideologically as well as genetically—but what disconnects you from billions of others.*]

6

Go Crusaders

A man with a gun walks into my eighth-grade classroom, talks for about fifteen minutes, and shoots. The entire middle school, fewer than eighty of us, is gathered in the room. The shot he fires is aimed at his temple. Here is a detail to intentionally color the scene: his charcoal beard slumps along with his body as he falls slack in front of the fifth graders seated at his feet. Tiny pinholes of blood form like a thumbprint at the crown of his head.

Then, the man, Mr. Adelaide, my eighth grade teacher, gets up, wipes his brow and says, "Folks, you've got to understand the consequences of the risks you take."

But I am leaving out details; some of which I can't recover from the gray archives in my head. He is not trying to kill himself. He looks menacing, crazy because here he is with details that fit and prove a menacing, crazy mood. He was giving a mini-sermon for the weekly chapel service held for the middle schoolers, and he wanted to make an impact. Mr. Ade believes in details, the shards of a moment that sink like shrapnel into the brain—fragmented images that haunt, that caution, that reveal.

The details I first notice are Mr. Ade's beard and glasses, and I'm trying to imagine what lies beneath them. His more permanent features like nose, mouth, and eyes seem to exist only to accompany and accentuate the beard and glasses. On my first day as an eighth grader, my mom takes a picture of me standing with the beard and glasses, then—more details—my bare arm chafes against his wool suit coat, which seems to give off as much heat as the September sun shining in the tall windows on the second floor of the middle-school building.

"Squeeze in more," my mom says, waving her free hand side to side. The beard pulls me into a full tweedy side-hug, and I realize that I am almost as tall as he is. I am closer to the beard than I anticipated. I'm no longer next to it; I'm experiencing it—a few whiskery tendrils brushing and bending across my cheek. I turn and look at his profile, my mouth slightly gaping in a kind of fearful surprise. The beard and glasses seem like some kind of barrier, and getting this close makes me feel improbably hot, sweat beading at the concave corners of my armpit. I try to force a smile, but all I feel is the air drying my exposed teeth, and the more I want to hazard a look up at Mr. Ade's face, the hotter everything gets. My mom snaps the photo.

"Bry, you weren't even looking! C'mon, lemme get one more." I stretch the smile into my face, cracking my lips at the corners, but I can't think of anything but the beard and glasses, that if I were to nudge his chin with my shoulder, hooks would rise off his ears and the whole beard would come off, only to reveal another mystic, gray layer.

"Ok, bud!" my mom says. "Have a great first day!"

I am suddenly aware of this moment where my mother is being motherly.

"And don't drink your Snapple 'til lunch time!" It's like she's reading lines of a play—inserting something mundane, asking the viewer to see her, know her.

"I know, I know." I know her.

"And don't forget to read your note!" She has been writing Hallmark-ish notes on my napkin ever since elementary school. I haven't read today's note yet, but because I'm familiar with the minutiae that make her my mom, I have a pretty good guess that it'll go something like, "After you're done munching your apple / be sure to wash it down with a strawberry Snapple!"

After my mother and other parents leave, homeroom begins, and all seventeen of my classmates and I gather at our desks, arranged in an angular U-shape, waiting for Mr. Adelaide to get up from behind his orange enamel desk and take his spot at the pockmarked wooden podium.

He steps slowly to the front of the room, almost stopping along the way to bow his head and touch the fingers on his hands to each other forming that geometric shape people use to pre-tell you that they have something measured and thought out to say. "Folks, you have a reputation," he opens, stepping to the podium and gripping the top edge of the gnarled wood with both hands as he speaks. "A very bad reputation. The teachers talk about you in meetings, saying you're the worst class the school has ever seen. I've spoken to your previous teachers. I know how you used to drive Mrs. Ogden to tears."

Inner heat pulses so strongly from my arms to my face that it takes on physical mass, the weight forcing my eyes down to the floor. It seems that a reputation is nothing more than a collage of collectively remembered fragments used to predefine someone, no interaction or experience required.

If my class has a bad rep, then I do, and therefore there are slices of my past that must be creating it. Here's what I can come up with:

- In fifth grade, I hung on the basketball hoop rim on the playground for longer than is allowed, and got a detention. *I am disobedient.*

- I keep my eyes open during prayer. *I am sacrilegious.*

- Levi brought in a *Hustler* in seventh grade, and I looked over his shoulder. *I am a pervert.*

- I wasn't the one that broke off the top to a one-armed desk and used it to paddle Joseph, who has been the brunt of everyone's jokes since he'd peed his white jeans in second grade. But I laughed at first. Then he dropped to his knees, and I saw his stunned eyes roll upward and hide beneath his blond hair. *I am too late.*

My reputation doesn't reflect the nights following where I'm in bed, sweating and thinking about the Bible verse that says, "Yes, each of us will give a personal account to God."

"But folks," Mr. Ade continues, "I'm going to forget everything I've heard about you starting right now. You're getting a clean slate—it's up to you if you want it to stay that way."

A second chance—thank God.

There was once a small window in the back wall of the living room, its glass framing a cropped image of where the side yard met the decaying fence that bordered our in-ground pool. But through the window, you couldn't see the pool; you could only know about it if you'd seen it from another vantage point, or if someone, such as me, had told you, "There, beyond that rotting fence, is a pool." One summer, when we are twelve, Paul and I do backwards dives and I spring off so far that I jump the border from deep to shallow; I break the water and my mouth hits the bottom of the pool, chipping off half of my front tooth. After climbing out, blowing words out through the new gap beneath my swelling lip, I tell my mother and Paul what happened and they spend the next two hours scanning the pool, looking for the missing piece—a tiny, white fragment floating in hundreds of gallons of blue-blurred vision.

Soon after my mom remarries in 1989, when I am six, the wall in the living room is dismembered and the skeletal planks of a new master bedroom, bath, and back deck are jointed into place. The room is unlike any in the rest of the century-old house; a flat, vacuous whiteness covers the new walls, ceilings, and closet doors. The older parts of the house are still plastered with yellowed, peeling patterns of wallpaper rooted to the floor by an evergreen shag carpet. Sunlight does not shine in these rooms, but is instead digested by the creeping dust and mildew. The new section, however, is draped in curtains of true light, falling in swollen shafts through a skylight that my new father keeps open as much of the year as possible.

Stepping from the collapsed threads of the green carpet over to the tight, candy-pink newness of their carpet, my head lightens. My parents refer to this room as "the addition," but it is really new growth, a tender shoot from the side of a decomposing stump.

"For the next month," Mr. Ade announces, "we will be learning about what a culture is." He tells us that the lesson will culminate with an archaeological expedition in the woods behind our building. He has buried remains in four separate areas, and each of us will be put into one of four groups, given a set of coordinates, and then let loose to dig up what remains we can find. At the end of the dig, we will come up with an assessment of what we think these people were like. For our homework, he tells us that we will practice this work by finding a trash bin somewhere, emptying its contents, listing the items, and making guesses as to how the owners live their lives.

"Mom, can I go through the trash in your bathroom?" I yell as I get home, dropping my blue lunch cooler on the deacon's bench, wondering what kinds of details are worth throwing away.

I am picking at a peeling corner of the wood-patterned linoleum that is shoddily glued to the top of my desk. As I wait for Mr. Ade to start the day's lecture, I study the contents inside. A CD by 2 Unlimited I am borrowing from and do not plan on returning to my cousin, and a copy of *Magical Mystery Tour* by the Beatles. Mr. Ade, sharing in my obsession with this band I've recently discovered, asked that I bring the album in so that he could play for the class the dissonant part at the end of "Strawberry Fields Forever" where, upon close listening, a low voice is heard saying, "I buried Paul." Mr. Ade suggests that it might also be saying, "cranberry sauce." I also see a returned math assignment that is marked, "100%! Excellent!" The sight of the jubilant red pen pricks my temples with the reminder that I let Levi show me the teacher's edition he'd somehow procured for the assignment.

I am a cheater.

Mr. Ade starts to write *Paradigm* on the board, like he has at the beginning of most of his lectures, but before he can add the ladle scoop on the *g*, a large man barrels into the room, stops, and points at Mr. Ade. "YOU!" he shouts. Like a battering ram, he charges at our teacher and plows him into the side of the wall. One of the wooden dowels on the low-hanging coat rack knocks his glasses off and he crumples to the floor. The large man looks up at us for a moment, then bolts out the room.

Mr. Ade gets up and dusts himself off. A few of us are muttering to each other about organizing a chase. None of us has ever been in a real fight before, but we hope adrenaline will be enough to avenge our martyred educator.

"Let's get him," says Steve. If the school had enough money for a football team, Steve would undoubtedly be named captain.

"Hold on," says a shaken Mr. Ade. "Let's write down what he looked like so we can describe him to the police."

"He's fat!" yells John.

"*Really* fat!" Steve adds.

"The fattest guy I've ever seen!" says John, not to be outdone by the class heartthrob.

"What color shirt was he wearing?" Mr. Ade asks.

"A plaid shirt."

"It was a blue turtleneck!"

"No, no, it was a green winter coat that was unzipped halfway!"

Mr. Ade: "You guys didn't really see him did you?"

"We just saw him!" yells someone.

"Ah, but you didn't *observe* him. There is a world of difference between seeing and observing. Just seeing will not do you any good, folks. What would we tell the police?"

We're stunned. None of us had a clue what he looked like. The door opens again, and a grey-haired man, heavier than Mr. Ade but not by much, walks in with a big smile. "C'mon guys—I'm not *that* fat, am I?"

At the end of the lesson, Mr. Ade swears us to secrecy—we can't tell the younger classes about his annual lesson in observation, lest they know what to expect. We join the enlightened ranks of the classes before us, classes that must now understand that the world is either apprehended or severely misrepresented by its details.

The bathroom in the addition is huge in comparison to the one-and-a-half others we are used to. Two pink sinks line the left wall, with a mirror above them that takes up the rest of the wall. Under the matching salmon towels that read *Jim* and *Barb*—a wedding gift—is a tiny wicker trash basket, lined with a plastic bag from Shaw's supermarket.

I turn over the bin and empty its refuse on the beige linoleum. Ninety-five percent of it is used tissues. At first I think the inhabitants must be sick, or have possibly just gotten over something. On closer inspection, I remember my nurse-mother's first question whenever she sees one of us blowing our nose: "Is there any color to it? If it's green or yellow, then you have an infection, and we'll have to get you some amoxicillin. If not, then it's probably just allergies." I write in my notebook:

1. Inhabitants must have allergies

I paw through the crusty clouds and find a Q-tip:

2. Inhabitants care about waxy build-up

A clear wrinkled Sunkist Fruit Gem wrapper:

3. Inhabitants are not putting the best candy in the bowl in the living room and keeping it for themselves

Final Assessment: *Inhabitants care about hygiene, but still make room for some occasional, high fructose fun.*

Looking in their trash is not really getting me very far. Here I can only tell who they are by what they get rid of, not what they deem worth keeping. If I focus on the tissues, what would they say about my mother that would change how I view her? Just because she is snotty doesn't mean she is *snotty*. What if details are distractions—the paper-light plunder of a meaningless crusade for insight?

I retreat upstairs to my room, and can't help but think that if I get hung up on the wrong thing, I'll get wildly off-track.

The world in front of me is zooming like a Seurat painting under a closing-in magnifying glass—*Sunday Afternoon on the Island of La Grande Jatte* becoming just a series of points, each one equal in size, but imbued with its own unique pigment. I could follow any one of them and get a story, but I don't know where to start, or which is the right story.

The objects in my bedroom seem to awaken from their silence, demanding that I speak their names, notice them on some level of significance I couldn't see before. The CD player: *Sony*. Closer, there is a glistening, rounded spot on the power button—evidence from the oily, repeated pushing of my right index finger. There is dust on the frequency dial because I am not listening to the radio—no, not just the radio, specifically 98.3 WLNH and 103.7 Peak FM—anymore, not since my cousin Zach told me to buy *Magical Mystery Tour*. "If you like that one," he said, "then I guarantee you'll like anything they've ever done."

I plug the wire end of a pair of large, padded headphones into the Sony-with-the-greasy-power stereo and cover my ears with them. They feel warm, as if they are melting earwax, and preparing my mind for a full ingestion of sonic details. I stamp my slick fingerprint on the power button and hear the CD start to spin like steady drops in a puddle; I move it to track six, "I Am the Walrus." The song warbles its way through the headphones, and I'm lying flat on my back and letting the music get stuck as it bounces from one earphone to the other—the sounds trapped, but still escalating. Near the end of the song, as John is scat singing his *goo-goos* and *chooba-choobas*, a dissonant chanting choir sets in from underneath the swelling cellos and stark snaps of the snare. It feels alive. The voices get louder, and though I'm getting more and more disoriented, I hone in on what I think they are saying. It could be anything, but I hear, *Look left, look left, everybody look left*, and I feel compelled to do so, hoping that what lies to my left, just out of sight, will reveal the rest of the story—why Mr. Ade is driven mad with details, who my parents are, why everything in my house save the addition feels like death. I yank my head left, but close my eyes—"look left, look left"—now there are other voices arising out of the mix. I open my eyes. A classical, thespian voice says what I hear as, *Dead? Are you dead, father? Rest, you,* but all that is in front of my eyes is a poster of Larry Johnson dunking a basketball against a shoddily rendered night sky background.

The song is fading, but a new, harsher voice enters, yelling, "Suck my dick!"

I jump so quickly that the headphone cord pulls from its socket and the voice fills the room. I hit *stop*, but it continues anyway. "If there are any hot girls out there—" I spin the volume knob and it's doing nothing, meaning the voice is either a demon or a Ham radio pervert piggy-backing my signal. If I pull the plug from the wall and the voice is still there, then it's a demon. I pull it; everything stops.

I'm dizzy, and not sure what to do with all this.

In the weeks leading up to the archaeological dig, we reach a chapter in our Christian-based history book about the Crusades. Generally, Mr. Ade doesn't really care for using the textbooks, calling them "tertiary" and saying they lack the ability to pull the reader into what was really happening. They focus too much on fact, not the bits that lead up to facts. He never assigns the static questions at the end of each section, deeming them simply "busywork."

But he is particularly interested in the series of nine Crusades carried out by sanction of the Pope in the Early Middle Ages. In order to make history come alive a bit, he breaks the class into research groups and assigns them one Crusade each. My group is given the less canonical Children's Crusade.

We are the Laconia Christian Crusaders. We share this mascot moniker with the local Catholic school in our area—the Holy Trinity Crusaders. "Go, Crusaders!" we yell at every season's sport games. There is even someone who occasionally dresses up as a knight and parades around our tiny gymnasium in regal splendor. In eighth grade, I share my classmates' pride in the Crusader identity; it conjures heroic images of Arthur and the

Knights of the Round Table. The idea that children played a part in what I can only guess was a great spiritual victory makes me excited to begin my research.

But things don't go so well.

The more specific data I dig up outside our textbook, the more it seems that the Crusades were the acts of desperately misguided people whose only talent was in convincing crowds to focus on large, impossible tasks. A detail that kills me: soldiers in the First Crusade resorted to eating the dead bodies of the Jews and Muslims whose city they had pillaged during the Siege of Maarat.

The Children's Crusade turns out to be one of the worst of the bunch. I had originally pictured the leader as some kid who had an uncanny ability to see and understand the world around him. Someone who, despite living in the midst of what would soon be called the Dark Ages, could bring divine light and clarity. My mind immediately called up a verse in the Gospel of Luke, where Jesus said, "anyone who doesn't receive the Kingdom of God like a child will never enter it." It was a radical statement in its time due to the low opinion of children held by the culture to which Christ made this declaration. Here was someone saying that what they wrote off as juvenile was not only poignant, but in fact necessary to understanding the nature of God. The smallest human was a revealer of the divine.

So, when I first encounter Nicholas of Cologne, a shepherd boy from Germany who attracted 7,000 followers to peacefully convert nonbelievers in Jerusalem, I think this kid's going to be the man.

Some of the newer encyclopedias I consult contest the existence of the Children's Crusade at all, saying that "children" was a mistranslation and that the stories passed down for centuries are just hearsay based on fragments of history—miniscule details that for some reason have outlived the broader truth and, over time, gained authority as universal fact.

It occurs to me that history is just a record of small things that later generations mistake as big things.

Nicholas's small thing starts as a herd of sheep. By 1212, he has traded in the sheep for a herd of 7,000 children that follow him over the Alps as they make their impossible way towards the Holy Land. The nagging, unresolved detail of the journey is the Mediterranean Sea—an inevitable roadblock that surely didn't escape their thoughts as they set out from Germany. Nicholas's answer? The sea would dry up for them. He turned his shepherd's crook into the staff of Moses, a symbol big enough to dupe thousands.

On the day of our presentations, the mood is noticeably dour. Group by group gets up and reports the same thing: some guy thought he was right; he wasn't, and lots of people died. Each time a new group reports on their topic, their faces look vaguely optimistic, a myth they can keep up at the beginning because the stories begin well enough and because we want things to make sense. We want to know why our school is named after an overwhelming swarm of murderous losers. But by the end of each presentation the class barely claps—the final sentences worthy of sackcloth and ashes, not applause.

"Nicholas thought he knew what was going on around him," I say during our turn. "But he didn't. He really, really didn't. They never even made it to the Holy Land." And it's true; the more updated sources report that the group—probably not even children, but rather "wandering poor"—either died on the way, were shipwrecked, or were sold into slavery in a foreign land. Those that reached the Mediterranean seemed genuinely surprised that the sea did nothing to greet them other than remain in place, and as a result, grew increasingly bitter at their misguided leader.

The mouth under Mr. Ade's beard looks pleased. We are reacting to history, not learning about it. I wonder where on earth we are going, and if we still believe that the distant impossible sea will open for us whenever our toes touch its first specks of sand.

In the woods behind our school, many of my classmates are finding mini civilizations, making grids of red elastic on the overturned detritus and topsoil. My group wanders around in awe of everyone's findings, but can't seem to locate the last spot—our spot. Even Mr. Ade starts wondering about the apparent lost city.

Their exhumed shards are taking shape, moving guesses to theories, stretching question marks into exclamations inside the head of each participating observer. I wander around with a trowel and a blank expression, stopping to dig wherever I am standing whenever Mr. Ade looks over at us. Leaves are tossed, roots and rocks, earwigs, larval clusters severed cleanly by the edge of the small shovel. I am a crusader, demanding findings that will validate the destruction I cause along the way.

With half an hour left on the last day of the dig, someone in my group yells, "Wait!" and we turn to see what has been unearthed: a broken piece of red plastic. We gather round, staring at its convex edges, brushing away dirt in hopes there is a word, a diagram on it to point us in any direction. "Gimme that!" someone yells, then just stares again, the act of touching the remnant not revealing anything. "Red, red, what's red," I'm repeating to myself, out loud at first, then silently, *what is red?* as if repeating the question will force an answer, the mere act of focused thinking somehow being enough to reconstruct a culture from a broken color. But what if this really is just trash, and not part of Mr. Ade's planted population?

"This might not be part of anything," I say. "We could just be wasting more time."

"No, no," says Mr. Ade, overhearing me and walking over. "You're on the right track. Just keep going." I want to believe him, but really, his methods—from the gun to the broken plastic—have taught me that evidence is fragmentary, that discoveries rarely yield anything but incomplete details.

The other groups have packed up their trowels, pieced together their findings, and prepare to head home and write their theories. We dig frantically, first with our tools, then our hands, and we find a few more pieces of red plastic that have no obvious pattern in common other than the fact that they are all red, made of plastic, and presumably fit together if all the right pieces are found. I look up and away from the plastic, my mouth slack and sucking air audibly as my eyes cruise the shapes and moving figures, each wearing their own on the sides of their sneakers and the hems of their pants, everything from the speck level on up having its own origin story. I haven't, and will never have, any idea who these people are.

[**Night** *clogs the gut of eternity, inflating the idea that you are created to praise something. Something is squirming, pressing from within, looking for an escape, and the longer it is trapped and swelling, the more rotten it becomes. But what is that canned heat, that puff of hot air? Perhaps it started as something nutritive, though force-fed: this desire to praise God, like an intravenous drip for someone who doesn't know they're thirsting to death. Someone slapped the crook of your elbow until a gorged, pumping blue vein rose to the surface, then they slid in an angle-tipped needle, combining its river with yours. But now the attendant has left, and what is flowing in is unending.*

It is said that if too much air clogs the hypodermic pathway, it will kill you, but if just a few tiny bubbles sneak in, they will just get reabsorbed. But what is the capacity for your blood to store dark, rising clouds?]

7

Wind of God

My first band is technically the worship team of Centre Harbour Christian Fellowship, in the days when attendance was moderate and there was not yet a desire to build a monstrous extra sanctuary. Instead of organs, pianos, and hymnals, we have guitars, drums, and a plastic crate full of simple, verse-chorus folksy songs typed up on acetate sheets that are projected on the wall for all to see. At almost four years old, I figure that being asked to play music with the adults means I must be swollen with talent.

Dinners with other church members are frequent, as are in-home concerts led by a brown, out-of-tune ukulele and me. My parents and other church folk, wearing flannel and drinking tea with honey, sit around our dark brown dining room table and make requests.

"Do you know 'This is the Day'?"

"Yes. Just give me a second to remember it."

I pause, look down at the instrument, and arrange the fingers on my right hand arbitrarily over the strings, then begin strumming wildly with my left hand, getting things backwards from the beginning. I know nothing about the song other than about how fast the tempo moves. I figure if I play loudly and sing quietly, no one will really notice my omissions, and I'll be able to deliver the feel of the song:

This is the day / this is the day / hmhmhm hm hm / hmhmLORD hm hm

The reception is so favorable that members of the worship team decide it would be fun/funny if I plucked and slapped at my four-string with them during Sunday morning worship services.

Dressed in a black-and-white, three-piece suit, topped off with a thick, dirty blond bowl cut, I sit on a stool in front of Lou's drum kit and strum along unamplified, having absolutely no clue what I am doing. I can't hear what I'm playing due to Lou's *boomchick*ing behind me, but this allows me to focus on the rhythm, and I try to match the movement of my hands with the pounding of his sticks on the snare. But when I get bored—even if it is in mid-song—I jump off my stool, put the uke on the floor, and walk back to where my mom, dad, sister, and brother are standing and singing along with the praise choruses.

Not long after I turn four, my dad hears that his esophageal cancer is progressing, and he senses he may not be around when I turn five, or see me outgrow my ukulele. So he drives me to Greenlaw's Music in downtown Laconia and walks me around the showroom of hanging guitars and stacked amplifiers. We come across a junior-sized, classical acoustic guitar, and he tells me that Rick, one of the musicians on the church worship team, will show me how to play it. "You're going to learn to lead the congregation in worship, just like Rick does," he tells me in a tone that seems more like a hopeful prediction than it does a parental mandate. When he buys the guitar, I'm oblivious to the fact that this is the last gift my father will give me.

There is a difference between "worship music" and "Christian music." Primarily, worship is for corporate gatherings on Sundays, at Bible studies, youth groups, and is not meant as entertainment. The music is a praise conduit as the worshiper seeks to make connections between the self and God. Outwardly, the person is part of the whole, and inwardly, they find a singular experience. Though a community worships together, "worship" is very much an independent act. Christian music, on the other hand, is created for entertainment, mainly for Christians. Because all of life cannot be spent in the safe confines of a church, many Christians have sought ways to create a culture with its own films, literature, greeting cards, and popular music. Worship music is a practice; Christian music is an industry.

The worship music that I grow up listening to is not the music that a Catholic, Lutheran, or other "high church" congregant uses in their services.

Their music represents ages of tradition, while nondenominational music primarily goes back to the 1970s, and is therefore distinguished from its ancient brethren as "contemporary worship" or "praise" music.

Contemporary worship is, like the independent tradition itself, often-times oversimplified in an effort to demystify hundreds of years of liturgy and make the content accessible and relevant to the hearer/singer. The songs are short, sometimes only two or three verses long, with a one- or two-line chorus that is created to be repetitive. A model example is the song by British band Delirious—who have vacillated between being a worship band and a Christian band—titled "I Could Sing of Your Love Forever." The chorus is the same as the song's title, meant to be sung over and over, and ends only at the discretion of the worship leader—the worship equivalent of a band's lead singer. Whenever we play this song, looping back to an open E chord again and again, it is hard for me not to think that we take a literal approach to the titular sentiment.

The music of worship songs is incredibly basic. Again, the idea is that anyone can sing these songs, and the only accompaniment one needs is an acoustic guitar. Even if the person cannot play guitar, the required skill level takes about three weeks of practicing basic chords to achieve. The music can, therefore, go anywhere a guitar does, and be played from memory.

The text typically lacks any sense of the awe and mystery associated with the more traditional hymn, and pretends that all is well with every-one's soul, all the time. Rather than the honesty of hymns with lines like, "Prone to wander, Lord I feel it / Prone to leave the God I love," we get songs like "Yes, Lord," whose Mobius-strip chorus is just a repetition of the title. I imagine that God is asking us mundane questions like, "Would you like more gravy?" *Yes, Lord.* "Does this shirt go with these slacks?" *Yes, Lord.*

These songs further assert our nondenomination, a movement that finds its roots in the Charismatic Renewal, sometimes known as the Jesus Movement, and that peaked in the late 1960s with hippies whose acid trips left them with heartburn. The movement focused on a return to simplicity and rejected the hierarchical nature of traditional denominations, often-times seeking individual "spirituality" rather than corporate religion. In a sense, hymns were seen as songs of the establishment, musically devoid of emotion. By combining a few simple chords with a couple of lines of biblical references, praise songs designed a minimalist framework to allow the worshiper space to be expressive. It wasn't the faith of their fathers—it belonged distinctly to them, and rarely reached beyond their immediate context. Over time, when the Jesus Movement's autonomous reaction became an establishment network of its own, church relationships strained and often led to church divisions and splits. They became so focused on finding distinctly personal worship experiences that they turned into slippery strands of butter-coated pasta—in the same pot, but unable to stick together.

✕

I show up at church one Sunday morning during my junior year of high school wearing tight, silver pleather pants. My family has been settled here at Laconia Christian Fellowship for four years—more or less since the Centre Harbour split. I have been playing guitar obsessively for two years, having started lessons at fourteen. A month after I started taking lessons, I was asked to join my high school's worship band since musicians were hard to come by in a school of fewer than 100 students, so it wasn't really a problem that I couldn't yet stretch my pinky to make a full G chord.

My pants reflect the sun so powerfully that their sheen is audible, and they retain so much heat that when I remove them, hot air rushes out like someone opening an oven to check on a spiral ham.

It is 8 a.m.—two hours before the service begins, but I am here early, as usual, along with the rest of the musicians and singers that make up Laconia Christian Fellowship's worship band. Every Sunday from 10 a.m.–11 a.m. we lead our congregation in the singing of worship songs.

After a few months of playing with the high school worship band, it wasn't long before word reached the team at the church, and Rick, now a worship leader at LCF after having migrated from Centre Harbour, asks me to join in the rotation. I agree to join, but I tell him that I'll only play the guitar, and that I'm not a singer.

"You know," he says, strumming a twelve-string, "The Lord doesn't care if a few of your notes are flat. If you're going to be playing up front with us, you really should be singing along, to set a good example for the congregation looking on."

It is a lecture I receive regularly. My mother often adds, "You, with your head down, just looking at your guitar. You look so sad up there!"

I try to tell them that even though I know I'm not trying out for heaven's choir, I like to think that God appreciates it when you realize your failings and adjust accordingly. What they do not understand is that I find the lyrics to these songs so self-absorbed that when I try to take them to heart, it feels as if I'm praising myself in my attempt to praise God.

Worship is a bloated word. Well, it is for most people I know. The only time it is used to connote something positive is in regards to church. At home or elsewhere, the word typically suggests some kind of unhealthy balance—you're not supposed to like anything *that* much unless it's God. "You two worship that TV," my mom says to Caleb and I whenever we are stuck in front of some show on Nickelodeon, sitting cross-legged like we are meditating, our heads angled up, our eyes drying because they've been forced open to receive the great light before us. "Turn it off and go play outside," she says.

"Right after the next commercial," Caleb says.

She pauses a moment, almost taken in by the bright animation of *Rocko's Modern Life*, but then wordlessly walks out of the room. When she comes back through ten minutes later, we haven't moved.

"I thought you said 'next commercial'?"

"Well, now the show's back on," I say. "And it's almost over, so we'll just finish it and then turn it off."

But at church, the word is repeated so often that I've stopped thinking of it as a verb and instead see it as some impregnable concept that everyone defines tautologically:

Q: What is worship?

A: It's when you worship.

The gleam of my silver pants does not catch Rick's eye when I walk into the school's gymnasium, where our church services are held. He is standing in the far corner, the back of his faded, charcoal suit facing me as he leafs through printout after printout in an aluminum standing file cabinet. Each sheet, arranged alphabetically, contains multiple copies of the chords and lyrics for hundreds of praise songs. He chooses the set each Sunday through prayerful reflection and musical sensitivity—the tempo of his selections should start *upbeat* and modulate song by song down to *meditatively slow* by the time the service has reached Communion—"prepare your hearts"

Rick says before the matzo crumbs and thimble-cups of white grape juice are distributed amongst the congregation.

Rick is like our lead singer. But we are not a band, he reminds us. Because he is still preoccupied trying to find a slow song in the key of D, our piano player, Candace, is the first to be blinded by my light. She is in the middle of thumping on a yellowed, slightly out-of-tune upright piano, practicing some praise song with her usual Muppet fury. She looks up, stops playing, and through wisps of her three-foot-long blonde hair yells, "Nice threads, man!"

"Thanks," I say through teeth that are as radiant as my shimmering legs, "I just got them this week." The loud exchange causes Rick to turn around as I'm setting my guitar down next to the drums.

"A bit much for church, don't you think?" he yells over.

"Maybe," I say, still smiling, trying to stave off the likely denouncement that I am breaking the unwritten, but upheld through stern looks dress code. "They're pretty cool, though, right?"

"I'm not sure that's how I'd put it. They look a little . . . distracting."

"Aw, c'mon Rick," says Candace, whose jeans, Birkenstocks, and thick wool sweaters speak to the '60s counterculture she still identifies with. "He's just being himself."

"Yeah," I say, encouraged by this adult's affirmation of self. "They're not supposed to be paying attention to me anyway. They're supposed to focus on the music."

"I don't know how you can *not* see those things from a mile away," he responds, all hints of mirth disappearing from his face. "I think it'd be best if you went home and changed. You can't stand up front in those things."

The rest of the team, Jesse, Paul, and Chris, put down their instruments and watch me talk myself into what has become a clichéd, but historically cyclical dialogue between my self-conscious misunderstandings of what exactly worship is, and the stiff-seeming faith of my father's generation. Despite their vehement overthrowing of centuries-old traditions, the struggle continues in the same old key: young people are "just not taking things seriously enough."

"But—I wear them in my band," I say, knowing full well it is a futile defense. "It's just my attempt at being an individual."

And the refrain: "This isn't a band, Bryan. It's not about *you*—we're simply the vehicles that allow each person a path into worship. They shouldn't be paying any attention to us at all."

His is an odd answer. The idea is that if anyone is focusing on me, they can't be focusing on themselves. It is ok for each person to become self-obsessed during this time, but it is almost sacrilegious to notice any details about the people that populate the room. I get it—Rick doesn't want my appearance to take people's focus off of their experience of worshiping God, but if pants can distract someone from the Creator of the universe, then perhaps we should be handing out Ritalin alongside the matzo and grape juice.

My glittering misstep cuts me deeper than I imagine it does those around me. I hoped the silver pants would be proof that I'm not spiritually dead—that there is vibrancy somewhere in between my lazy gaze and fretting fingers. On the few Sundays where I am standing with my family and not playing guitar during worship, I grow increasingly awkward and anxious. All around me people stand with reverential eyes closed and/or lifted hands that turn them into solitary vessels of spiritual confinement. They are like sleepwalkers, and I never know what they will do next.

The praise that rises out of their fingertips applies pressure to my motionless body—my sin of mobile omission. I am not doing my part. I try to mouth the line of a verse, but only hear a drone that grates against the communal key. God may not dwell on how bad I sound, but I'm having a few problems getting past it.

My mom whispers, "You can close your eyes, you know. No one will pay attention to how you're worshiping." But she must be paying attention to how I'm worshiping if she's noticing that my eyes are open—meaning that her eyes are also open, and now it's not just me who's suffering from my failed attempts to tap into the divine. By not doing *anything*, I feel their stares through closed eyelids. "Look how we don't care!" they say. "We're worshiping in spirit and in truth! With reckless abandon! Social conventions mean nothing to our genuine hearts!"

"Would you please all find your seats as we enter into a time of worship?" Rick asks, as he does at the beginning of every service. Though I missed most of the practice, I was able to drive home, change into jeans, and get back to my guitar just before Rick makes his announcement. The dozens of disparate conversations among parishioners catching up on the previous week splinter around me. They talk about how "work was a real bear this week," or, "Jenna still isn't responding to the antidepressants—could you keep praying, though?" or, "my zucchinis are huge this year! I brought some so you can make your relish." The chats are mini liturgies that seem as vital as the times we gather and sing.

This morning's opening song is "Come, Now Is the Time to Worship." The song seems to celebrate the time for worship, but doesn't really offer any direction as to what that time entails. In a more traditional church, services start with an invocation, or call to worship—a brief reading or chanted phrase that shifts the people's vision from temporal individuality to the eternity of corporal community, the words like a divining rod held aloft in search of holy validation.

However, this worship song stops time, saying, here we are, we are worshiping right now. But just by repeating the chorus over and over, does that mean that I actually am worshiping? What is now? Right now I am playing the chords of this song, and trying to find a new way to pluck a D to a D suspended every time we circle back to the beginning of the song, even though we've been through it twice already. The song is more of a series of false starts that says, "Ok, this time, we're really going to worship. Ready . . . *now*."

I want my guitar part to sound like U2's "Still Haven't Found What I'm Looking For," so I jump to the higher register of the neck, playing arpeggios that plink polyrhythmically, adding ninths and fourths over the staid, basic chord shapes that everyone else on the worship team is playing. If I am thinking of how the Edge would play this song, then I am not worshiping. Or, am I accidentally worshpping the Edge, because it is he that I'm think-ing about in the *now* that everyone is singing in, inhabiting, each blindly dowsing for our own version of God?

Since the song offers me no directions on how to worship, except that now is the time for it, I feel as if I'm wasting time, as if I am some amateur avant-garde exhibit of performance art, standing motionless on a bare stage holding a hammer and repeating steadily and without inflection, "I am hammering. I am hammering."

The second line of the song moves into the second person voice, invit-ing a "you" to the worship experience. Who is the you? The usage seems to be somewhat mythical, a clever trick to hide what our closed-off body language is saying: *I'm* worshiping, so please leave me be, arms up like curtains and eyes clasped to bring the focus inward; and please don't wear any bright, reflective clothing that might distract me from my personal worship experience. On stage I am keeping my head down so that I don't have to look at others worshiping, standing there swaying to their soul's metronome, and me left wondering what is inside them, and why it hurts to try and bring my head up or shut my eyes. The weight of worship builds like a swarm of air inside me, a paradoxical emptiness that spreads, inflating until I am bloated, filled with the fear that, perhaps, nothing is in there.

A few weeks later, our worship team piles into Candace's minivan and we drive south to Peterborough, New Hampshire, to attend an annual worship summit. Churches from all over New England send their musicians to the summit each year in order to spend a long weekend attending workshops on such topics as incorporating interpretive dance into worship services, effective tambourine handling, and tips on the latest software for lyric projection. At the end of each day's itinerary, all the groups gather in the main sanctuary for an extended time of worship, led by some of the bigger names in the industry—celebrities that pose an odd paradox to Rick's vehicle theory. It means, in any case, that I must stand in the audience with a crowd of professional worshipers. There will be no way that I can reside with my hands in my pockets and not be talked to about my lack of participation.

As this is our second time attending the summit, we've established certain traditions; one being dinner at a tiny Italian restaurant near the church. The restaurant is situated in a large, white New Englander; the owners reside in the back, serve their customers on the first floor, and operate a folk instrument shop on the second. Though the shop was closed when we arrived last year, they opened it for us and let us pluck a few nylon-stringed acoustics, banjos, autoharps, and fiddles.

For dinner, I settle on a dish called Buttero's Chicken. While the Tuscan term actually refers to a type of shepherd, here it refers to the heavy-handed portions of butter and garlic that engulf and cook thinly pounded chicken breasts. The low-cal, diet-lite-saccharine-margarine food I am normally served at home is nothing like the richness I have just ordered. Despite the gastronomic otherness of Buttero, I jump at the chance to try the bold, full-fat flavor. When the dish arrives, the fillets are floating on top of silk scarves of fettuccine in the soft glow of a light roux. The meat is so tender and lubricated that a relaxed throat is really all it takes to swallow—just looking at this dish prompts twinges of acid reflux at the base of my rib cage. Globs of hastily chewed chicken and pasta are soon sliding down like Viking war ships, paddles churning circles into a whirlpool of indigestion.

When the bill arrives, I hear a faint watery gulp in my stomach—a noise I attribute to the second Shirley Temple I ordered along with dinner and finished in two long pulls after devouring the chicken. But the noise increases in volume, and it begins to feel as if someone has attached a basketball pump to my stomach lining and started pumping until the black, rubber seams begins to crack.

I need to let the air out in the worst way, and so before climbing into the van, I leisurely walk around the perimeter of the restaurant, strategically pretending to be interested in the landscaping on the far side of the house.

"Hurry up!" Candace yells. "We're late to the worship service as it is!"

Good, I think; a few more minutes where I don't have to feel the pressure of praise from all sides.

When we get to the parking lot of the church, I step out last, letting my stomach begin its paratrooping descent. I watch to see which direction each person walks around the van, and I choose the opposite path, and take another flora detour over by the edge of the parking lot. We can hear the tinny strums of acoustics plugged into direct-in outlets, and the dull thump of a mic'd bass drum.

"C'mon! We're missing the good stuff!" says Candace, as she breaks into a Birkenstock trot.

"Oh yeah?" I ask with a reluctant crane of my neck, releasing a bit more nervous pressure before running to join them. But as I reach the glass double doors, Buttero puffs me up again. "I have to run to the bathroom; I'll meet you guys in there." I didn't want to have to use my one bathroom card already, as I usually save it to help waste some time in the middle of the long-winded service.

I head down the dark hallways that have been closed off for the evening itinerary, knowing that no one will be using the restrooms towards the rear of the building. The swelling pain is intense, and the pounding of the drums and djembes from the sanctuary allows me a longed-for opportunity for an authoritative, auditory release. I figure this has to be the end of the intestinal distress, and resolve to go stand awkwardly with my team.

They are situated close to the front row on the right side of a packed and sweaty sanctuary; guitar chords and repeated lines of praise are echoing atop raised hands and lifted hearts. I sidle my way through brown, leather-padded chairs and Spirit-filled worshipers, and no sooner do I take my coat off then I am filled with an unholy spirit. I need an exorcism, but of a variety that the worship leaders here are not quite equipped to carry out.

If I try to leave again, I'll get another talking-to about how I should be taking these services more seriously. "That's why we're here," they'll say. "To receive an anointed touch from the Lord." Then they will try to get me to sing, lest I be perceived by those around us as spiritually empty. At this point, I'd speak in tongues in order to feel empty.

Gary Sadler, the evening's guest worship leader, finishes the song "Heart of Worship" and uses a series of arpeggios to segue into his song, "Wind of God." I gasp—God is clearly not letting me suffer my inner turmoil without driving home some unbelievable symbolism. I don't know if it's my nerves or some deeper cosmic judgment, but the song and the pressure inside my body reach their peak at the same moment, and I have no choice but to start deflating slowly, hoping no one will notice. As a deflection, I start singing, much to the pleasant surprise of Jesse and Rick standing on either side of me. "Spirit come like a mighty wind!" I belt out with distracting conviction. When I let go of myself, Gary leads us in the line "Come and blow \ wind of God \ Blow wind of God."

As he carries out the "awwwd" syllable in melodic melisma, Jesse's eyes—closed in worship—pop open and turn in my direction. I'm already looking at him in horror. He nudges Chris and whispers to him—he stares, laughs, and then whisper-laughs to Paul. This continues down the line until the whole group has figured out the source of the other spirit lying heavy in the room. Chris taps Jesse on the shoulder and motions for him to turn around—they immediately buckle with laughter, clutching at their stomachs in the same way that I am. I turn to see what the matter is: the seven rows behind us, once elbow to elbow, are totally vacant.

With that, I give up and walk out in a kind of narcotized peace, knowing I have nothing left to give.

[**Light** *beams are clouded with the tar blown from a mouth that is drying, a ridgeline of spit turning slowly into glue and fusing the lips permanently in the pursed position, looking like the* o *in* doubt. *The smoke chains seem to always be exhaled, leaving the room suffused with the pungent, burnt mist of nicotine. The words of your mother repeat,* It's cancerous, It's cancerous, *while that word of your father,* cancer, *sticks like spit to your sense of belief. It's as if that death swell hanging in the air knows that you can't hold your breath forever.*

Inhale the sun-stung smoke; when you breathe out, what will be left?]

8

A Desperate Blowing of Smoke

Ten minutes ago I was making out with Natalie in a green, fifteen-passenger van, filled to its capacity. Guys and girls are not allowed to sit in the same row on outings led by Laconia Christian High School, so I sit in the far back corner and she in the row ahead of me. It is March in the year 2000, she is a junior to my senior, and we are both en route to preach the good news to the homeless in NYC. Her torso is twisted and leaning backwards, while my back arches forward. We are Chagall's lovers stuck in a van. I had made a mental pact with myself to not kiss her until we were "official," but there is so much steaming life passing between us that I can't even think straight. Somehow, the chaperones, one of which is my mother, don't seem to notice. In mid-slurp—we're both pretty new to this sort of thing—I wonder why anyone would pick me to be their Savior.

A few hours later, I am Jesus. Stevie and Mel, the husband-and-wife team that leads these missions trips to New York City, want me to paint my face white, dotted with two red hearts on my cheeks. I adamantly refuse the makeup, afraid it will collect with sweat and seep into the corners of my eyes, stinging and reminding me that my face is covered in makeup. I acquiesce to their chosen robes of glory: a dull white T-shirt with pits darkened like a sun and a moon rising out of a smoky white light. My borrowed, stiff white jeans bend only at the knees. I hand my tortoise-rimmed glasses to my mother, and this giant city that I am visiting for the first time blurs at the seams, the crisp lines of dark and light smudging to weeping ash.

On the corner of 52nd and Lexington, or some other New York-ish convergence, skyscrapers bend with the curve of the earth over my head like an ambush descending. A hot, militant air exhales from subway stairs that go down, down, down, carrying with them dozens of heads turned away from us. Stevie pulls me aside, warning me to watch out for some sect of people identified by tan pants. "They hate Christians," he says. "They'll stick you with a knife in broad daylight."

Everyone is suddenly wearing tan pants, and without my glasses, idle briefcases and coiled umbrellas are shields and machetes. I try to rub out the cataracts of a cloudy holy war and focus on remembering my interpretive dance moves.

Fingering a few extra packs of D batteries in his parka pocket, Stevie hits play on a bulky tape/CD boombox. The late Keith Green's ghostly instrumental piece "Prodigal Son" haunts out of the speakers; its scratchy recording quality heightened and thinned by the New York noise it becomes a part of. With godlike solemnity, I look up, lift one arm, then the other, towards heaven, and begin miming God creating the world. I materialize and throw stars into place, and I let there be light. I separate the heavens from the earth with a heel spin and outstretched palm. I shape and bring forth plants and animals, then glide in a circle, smiling as I survey my creation—an Eden that is rife with the too-sweet smell of roasting nuts and staring faces that dare me to say *it is good*.

The music swells and cracks as I turn to create human life. Natalie is crouched in a ball, her face an inch from the pebbled sidewalk as I approach her. With patting motions, I make a human the way a six-year-old forms a mud pie. With the lightest graze, my palm touches her back—her cue. She pulses, rolls, and becomes Homo erectus. Her white shirt echoes my divinity while her black pants show that she is an individual and has the capacity for free will.

Her character is that of the Seeker, the representative of all mankind who will, in the course of this street drama's performance, accept me as her Savior, then turn to a series of earthly vices, only to be left heartbroken and in my arms. The world will impair her vision, over and over. As we dance, people come up out of the subway tunnel. They don't even pause to consider walking around us, but instead just stroll through, effortlessly finding a hole as Natalie and I pirouette away from each other. They are not fazed, as if to say that if there weren't white teenagers convinced that dancing could save souls, *that* would truly be worth noting. Unlike me, Natalie does not refuse the face paint, and the smell of sweat and chemicals as we twirl to an offbeat box step is the only thing keeping me from pulling her in to a full-on, holy French kiss.

"I have to buy really hard-core porn to get it up, Mr. Parys," says Andrew after sipping a pint of Stella Artois, his sixth or seventh of the evening. Normally, we'd be drinking real ale in a quiet pub on the canal, but they all closed at 11 p.m. in the sleepy hill town of Lancaster, England. The only way Andrew, Rob Ward—a professor of ours at St. Martins College—and myself can get a drink at this hour is by sitting in a back room in one of the town's night clubs. We settle on the Revolution, a neon-red-and-black dance club that boasts one hundred flavors of vodka shots, including bubble gum and Thai chili, at £5 each. Instead, we go for the overpriced Belgian lager.

Andrew is a thirty-five-year-old enrolled in the college's English and creative writing program. Being that I am an international college student studying abroad during my junior year and he is, what the British call, a *mature* student, we frequently find ourselves on the outside of most conversation circles before and after classes. He is a chain, no, chainsaw smoker. When he's not breathing one in, he's busy rolling Drum tobacco into his next smoke. The mechanized ritual highlights the rusty bumps between his index and middle fingers, due to years of Drum and writing longhand. He has written a novel, he tells me, but has not typed a draft since he contracted tendonitis close to a decade ago.

"I can't get through eight hours of sleep without getting up twice for a cigarette and a coffee," he says in his deep but lilty Northern drawl, pulling on the words like drags of his cig. I picture myself putting a dry cigarette between sticky morning lips, and in so doing choke up a blob of Stella. Techno remixes pound around our heads. Seated on a faded, black leather couch, we lean back frequently to stay out of the way of Axe-doused British boys buying bubble gum shots for girls who dance as if they are hoping their tiny tops will fall off as much as the guys hope for that same outcome.

The conversation has left Rob and me mostly speechless as we try to meet Andrew's deep gaze. I am mostly focusing on the sticky couch, the dark gray creeping through the black hair shrouding Andrew's temples and the soul patch under his chin. When a guy tells you that in order to have sex with his wife, he needs to muster up the courage to buy the filthiest backroom porn he can find due to the side effects of his antidepressants, words have a way of sticking to your tongue like hairy strands of loose tobacco.

$$\times$$

A few weeks prior to my divine appointment in NYC, I sit in Evangelism class at Laconia Christian School. It is the only Christian education elective I have not taken in my four years of high school, by my own fear-driven design. It is my last semester before graduation, and there are no other electives available that I haven't taken twice, let alone once. There's no way around it this time. I'm going to have to learn to save people.

Over the course of the semester, the class covers the basics of how to talk to strangers about Christ, and ultimately, lead them in what is called the Sinner's Prayer—a series of words that, when others repeat them with us, mean that they are part of God's fold. Though we are not given a script, the goal is to prepare us for the class final: a weekend trip to the unsaved streets of New York City.

Stevie and Mel teach the class as well as organize and lead the trip. For LCS and for its sponsoring church, Laconia Christian Fellowship, they are our resident missionaries. In addition to annually leading a handful of trips to NYC, Armenia, the Dominican Republic, Romania, etc., they also serve as our unofficial youth pastors.

They have been hosting a youth group at their house for some time now, and most of my friends attend. I have heard that there is a lot of pressure to be overly spiritual—speak in tongues, prophesy, that sort of thing. I have never been part of a youth group, but I've heard that you get to talk to the person you have a crush on while bowling or mini-golfing.

Stevie and Mel's group isn't like that. In fact, from what I can tell, theirs is a reaction against those spiritually soft kinds of youth group. They're serious about spiritual development, and they want everyone there to be what is referred to in our nondenominational circles as "baptized in the Holy Spirit," through which comes tongues, prophecy, and other gifts of the Holy Spirit. But these sorts of things frighten me. Not only is there the looming fear that I am not spiritual enough to actually perform these feats—they tell me these are the marks of true followers of Christ—but I don't like speaking in public of any kind, especially if it's in tongues—some mishmash of improvised Hebrew that no one, often including the speaker, understands.

In my head, Stevie and Mel have targeted me for their proselytizing wiles. I can't help but project on them my own fears of the shortcomings of my so-called faith. Up until this point in high school, I feel as if I'm a Christian—maybe even a good one at times. I tithe 10 percent of my earnings from my job as a sandwich artist at Subway, and I play guitar on the worship team at church and school on a weekly basis. And these things feel good, sometimes soul satisfying even.

But then my best friends return from meetings at Stevie and Mel's and they speak about it like some secret society, complete with its own set of linguistic standards. They make these hazy, unrecognizable faces and sideways smiles to other members when they talk about it around me, as if to say, "You wouldn't understand; you've only been baptized through *water.*"

Stevie has asked me to join their group a number of times, but I've always responded in some semi-verbal negative groan that he may or may not perceive as a poor man's tongues. I always look down when he's talking to me, looking up occasionally to see his full-bearded face is smiling in a knowing way.

So, after one of the first few classes of the semester, when Stevie pulls me aside and asks me again to come to youth group, finishing it this time with, "And, oh—we're announcing the roles in this year's drama next class," I have trouble meeting his eyes.

Every time we sit and have coffee, it's the same old thing: *why do you believe in God?*

Andrew and I are always early for our creative writing class at St. Martins, so we've taken to just meeting at the JCR—a campus coffee shop by day and dance club, complete with subsidized drinks, by night. Back in New England, smoking has been banned at almost every place that has a ceiling, but here in the old country, pubs and clubs wouldn't be proper without a brown-and-gray mist floating like burst thought bubbles above everyone's heads.

Andrew's orange fingers are already tugging at a hand-rolled cigarette when I walk in and set my backpack down. His face, grizzled with graying stubble, is fixed on me, and he seems paused, not even breathing. I squint and lean in a bit after he doesn't answer my "Hey, Andrew." He purses his lips like a face on a totem pole and blows a dense cone of smoke in my face, causing me to fall back in my seat, choking, waving my hand, and shaking my head—my whole body repulsing with a *no no no*. Andrew laughs as hysterically as his nicotine-slackened frame lets him.

"Christ, Mr. Parys, you are such an easy target," he says, one hand adjusting the thickly wrapped kaffiyeh around his neck, the scarf's threaded ligaments browning more each day. He knows it bothers me when he says *Christ* like that, so casually, and when I ask him to not say it around me, he giggles like a preteen. So, I've taken to just shaking off the spike of heat that flashes in my head when the name is intoned.

"That's so disgusting. You know I'm allergic."

"Oh for fuck's sake; everyone's allergic to smoke, Mr. Parys. Everyone knows it's terrible for you." He never calls me by my first name, his more formal moniker being some mix of pedantry and camaraderie.

"Then you know more than anyone that it's time to quit," I say, sounding more like my mother than planned.

"I used to think that," he continues, his eyes moving up sideways as if he is entering some long, dark tunnel that is always just outside his periphery. "But then, when I was a busker, it was just something all the other homeless musicians did. After Australia, it became the only thing I looked forward to."

"Yeah, well, my grandfather felt the same way. Then he talked through a hole in his throat for the last years of his life."

"You're such a good Christian boy, Mr. Parys," he says, chuckling again and sending another puff my way. The cloud is viscous, and I can't see him or anything for a second. Our conversation can't go anywhere but here. Every time we talk, he brings up my faith, makes fun of it in his own doubting Thomas way, and then grills me on every possible issue relating to it. The way he says words like *Bible, Jesus, spirituality*, makes them sound so silly, so illogical. "I don't know why you're still trying to see him anyway."

"But I do see him," I say, the familiar words climbing out of my throat without me even thinking of it. "Well, not literally, but . . . like you see the wind."

"Oh, really? So, when do you see him?"

"All the time." As soon as I say it, it feels disingenuous. I don't *see* God all the time, nor do I think anyone, even the most spiritual of people, do. St. Francis couldn't have been in constant connection to his Maker, because isn't that what makes us human and not angels—the desire to see God through an impenetrable celestial fog? St. Frank had to pee, Billy Graham brushed his teeth, and C. S. Lewis felt abandoned by God when his wife, Joy, passed away after only three years of marriage.

But, *all the time* is the answer I was taught to give during high school. God is omnipresent. Faith is the evidence of things unseen. The words of the song "Mind's Eye"—by the popular Christian band DC Talk, who started out like a religious version of the Beastie Boys, and ended up like an even more religious U2—ring in my head, something about God's presence being proved by the trees' leaves blowing in the wind.

"Look at the trees outside," I continue. "The leaves—that proves God is there, uh, here."

"And how is that, exactly?"

"Because he created it!"

"Did he? What if he didn't?" The smoke is gathering again, his words fusing and falling out of it like the cloud is speaking and he's just its smoldering marionette. "Even if he did, he checked out a long time ago. Just because the trees are still here, doesn't mean he is."

"Well . . ." I say, looking down and to the side a few times, picking up my coffee and finishing it in one long pull. I bring it down, and then back up even though it's empty, and then I'm staring at the soiled brown ring in the crevice at the bottom of the cup—a circular remnant, a reminder that something once filled this cup. "I don't know. I don't know if that's right."

Andrew's shoulders rise and fall, a chuckle and a *hmph* all at once. Every answer I have doesn't convince him, but everything he says is making me more and more nervous. He's not shaking my faith so much as he's exposing that I've never put it into my own words, only the lines that I've rehearsed my whole life. If I said that I saw God all the time at my church at home, heads would nod and mouth *That's right, amen.* No further questions—pure belief that is unfiltered and less filling.

If I said "amen" to Andrew, he'd do that shoulder chuckle again. In my freshman year at the Christian college I attend, save this year abroad, I learned in Old Testament Survey that one of the Hebrew roots of the word amen is *Emunah*, which can be translated to mean "to agree." But like most of ancient Hebrew, the meanings usually stem from something physical, real. In this case, it means, "to lift up in support of." Roof beams, wheel spokes, food—*manna*—all say *amen.* When Moses was holding his staff up in order to part the Red Sea, he had to keep it raised for hours upon hours. His brother Aaron came to his aid and helped him keep his arms up, through *emunah.*

Amen: to hold you when you're about to pass out.

My arm falls slack and lets the cup back down to the table, and the smoke is getting worse. Class is in five minutes, but I'm afraid Andrew only needs another thirty seconds to completely dismantle my apology for faith.

"You just . . . you just believe, Andrew. That's all I can say. You're just too bitter to believe. You're making it more complicated than it needs to be."

"More complicated! I'm not making anything more complicated, for Christ's sake! I want to believe, believe me. More than anything. *He's* the one making it complicated!"

"God wouldn't do that," I say without thinking, making it sound as if God's an old buddy and someone just told me he got caught stealing an apple.

I grab my empty cup again to shut myself up, and I notice our friend Dominic coming in to grab a coffee before class.

"Hey, Dom!" I yell, scrambling awkwardly, causing Dom to cock his head to the side.

Andrew exhales, and I can't catch my breath.

Today's Evangelism class is a special one: the day Stevie and Mel descend the holy mountain and reveal the parts for the *Doors* drama team. The feeling is similar to awaiting word on who would get the lead in this year's performance of *Oklahoma!* but we don't audition in the normal way. Instead, Stevie and Mel pray about it for weeks, waiting to hear from the Lord who would play who.

The main roles in the drama besides Jesus and the Seeker are a series of players that represent the temptations a godless world could offer a human. Each stands behind a different door waiting for the Seeker's curiosity to get the better of her. Door #1 is a material girl—the allusion to Madonna I'm assuming has to be on purpose—and represents the love of possessions and wealth, fancy sports cars, expensive clothes, and an endless supply of makeup. Door #2 is a drug addict, though the way the character is mimed, there is no desperation or implied train wreck, and so the "addict" connotation isn't quite right. This person loves drugs, plain and simple, and symbolizes the option to achieve happiness through herbs and needles. Door #3 reveals the playboy—the wine-and-diner that swing dances into your heart, then your bed, instantaneously leaving you with an unwanted pregnancy.

The playboy then brings the Seeker to a clinic, and a procedure is mimed behind a black curtain with red letters that read: "Abortion." The emotional distress of Door #3 leads to the final door: suicide—played by two black robed figures that, despite not looking it at all, are meant to appear comforting. When the Seeker gets swallowed in their embrace, they quickly don skull masks and attempt to kill her, but she is saved at the last moment by Jesus—who up to this point has been off to the side, having been murdered and lately risen again.

The roles of Jesus and the Seeker were not, as one might think, handed out to the most spiritual of candidates, but rather tended to be the quieter, more awkward kids of the group. My own read of the situation is that quiet and awkward are signifiers of the spiritually disadvantaged. The less you take part in class, the higher the chances of becoming the Chosen One.

After rattling off the smaller roles, Mel pauses for the big announcement.

"And our new Savior will be . . . Bryan Parys!"

I'm numb with fear, and some odd form of excitement that I don't understand. A groggy "What?" is all that seeps through as everyone around me is staring.

"Your Seeker will be Natalie Robinson," she then beams, in an attempt to cut through the frozen twitch my face is holding, "You're her Jesus!"

Natalie has been driving to my house after school to practice our moves for the drama. Both of us think we are desperately in love with other people, and bring up our unrequited frustrations to each other more than I expect.

"His parents won't let him date anybody," she says. "They're really strict."

"I have the opposite problem," I say, pouring us lemonades. I notice that my mother has left an open bottle of a strawberry-kiwi wine cooler in the fridge, and with a rebellious grin, I grab it and pour a drop in each glass. We giggle, thinking about how *crazy* we're being. "Lizzy's parents love me. They've all but begged her to go out with me. She's the problem." I get self-conscious talking about this with Natalie, and for some reason want to change the subject. "Yeah, so. Hey—you've been on these kinds of trips before; what's it like talking to a homeless person about God?"

"Weird. It's really weird. You never really know what they're going to say, or if they'll even talk to you when you say 'Hi.'"

"The thought of it gives me the creeps. I mean, I know the Bible says we should tell all the nations and whatever, but this seems like a really weird way to do it."

"I guess it's not for everybody."

"That's what I'm afraid of. There's no turning back now—in a couple weeks I'll definitely be in a place where I'll have to talk to someone about Jesus."

"The one time that sticks out to me the most was when I was on a trip last year over Christmas. We were in this bus terminal, and it was so bright. I remember that because I thought it was so weird that we were there looking for homeless people at the bus station where they were trying to get warm. Normally we always went out at night, finding people under blankets and stuff."

I'm staring at her, a sip of lemonade still pooled under my tongue; the thought of looking for people under blankets is making me forget how to swallow.

"I was with a couple of other people talking to this one guy, and for some reason everyone left but me," she continues. "The guy looks at me, smiling, but he says, 'You're going to preach to *me*? You're so young and safe. I can't even go across town to get to one of the shelters or I'll get beat up. I can't take the coats that you guys give out 'cuz someone will jump me and steal it.'"

She pauses and looks down. "As I walked away, I was like, 'What the heck can I say to these people that'll actually help? I don't know anything about anything!'"

"If I weren't so frightened—" I say, a cough of lemonade interrupting, "—of what they'd say, I feel like a better way to go about it would be to just ask them to talk about whatever they feel like, and we could just listen."

Andrew is telling us about his twenties. He was a classically trained Spanish guitarist—used to practice eight-plus hours a day. The two recordings he's given me prove his worth. Flawless, fluid arpeggios—he sounds like a quartet. He gets so into the pieces that, halfway through a song, I can hear his breathing pick up until it snorts in rhythm with the bass line he plucks with his right thumb.

He was so good, he says, that he was offered a chance to go to the States and study under a contemporary of Andrés Segovia. His girlfriend at the time told him to put it off for a year and go busk around Australia. He did. According to him, the increased humidity swelled his overzealous hands and tendonitis stole close to 70 percent of his speed and ability.

"That's when I gave up on him, Mr. Parys, and replaced it with cigarettes and Prozac. Those at least keep me up." Well, *most* of him, I almost say.

Rob, who loves early Harold Pinter plays, takes this moment to reveal, in his quiet, marbled tone, that he's an agnostic. They both take bubbly gulps, lean forward, and look at me. They know I'm a Christian, and both suggest by the confession of their belief systems that they want me to explain myself.

The mission house in NYC where we take up our lodging comprises three floors of adaptable space. The building sees a new team of small-town revivalists almost every weekend. On the second and third floors, mattress pads and sleeping bags are strewn like shuffled-off skins. The ground floor is a large kitchen set with folding tables. In the back are bins of donated coats, socks, and toothbrushes.

The night we arrive, it's decided that we will refresh ourselves with one round of the ham sandwiches that volunteers spend afternoons layering in coolers, then hit the streets to let the newbies talk to a few homeless people.

We climb into the van and roll off into an already dark night.

Stevie trawls the streets slowly—he knows the hotspots, but he doesn't want to miss any stragglers.

"There's one!" my friend Ian yells from the backseat. Stevie stomps the brakes.

"Ok—go go go!" The door slides open and three or four Christian soldiers move onward, armed with jackets and sandwiches, and descend on the sleeping homeless, rousing them from beneath their cocoons of wool blankets.

"Aren't you coming?" says Ian.

"I'll sit this one out."

"Bryan, seriously. You have to do this. You're being selfish; let's go." He tugs my arm; I pull back. "You need to grow up. You'll never learn anything if you don't get out and try this." He turns and hops onto the sidewalk. "You disappoint me."

✕

The seven beers affect me more heavily than theirs do, my twenty-year-old body having never really drunk until England, save the occasional drops of a wine cooler. I don't usually talk about my faith. Unlike the beer I've seen people like my uncles drink until they're slouched and burpy, British ale makes me hazily reflective. If ever I was ready to talk about God, it was at this point.

I start talking.

"It's all about Mystery; capitalized, y'know?" They don't seem to know. "Well, what I mean is, if God revealed himself to me in an obvious way, I probably wouldn't have faith in him. I mean, would you put faith in someone who revealed themselves to you?" They don't laugh. They are not letting me deflect.

"Right before my dad died, he left a tape for us," I continue, not really sure why I default to this. I realize that in the year I've been in England, I've not mentioned my father's death to either Andrew or Rob, and it feels awkward to sort of save this detail for the big finish. "He had wanted to become a pastor, but it was clear he wouldn't realize that dream. So he preached a sermon to his family saying that, 'If God told me to walk into a fiery furnace, I'd do it.' He had a faith that earned him a place alongside the Old Testament prophets.

"I've spent my life in search of that deathbed fire. And I don't think I have it. But I think God's ok with that for now."

I pause, thinking I've gone too far. The thrum of the metronomic bass kicks the floor beneath us, a whorl of smoke, pickup lines, and clinking glasses makes me question whether or not the words I've grasped for did in fact materialize. And yet, their gaze doesn't stray from my face. I wait for a question, any hint that they've even heard me. I keep puffing out these words, but by the time the vocal shards hit my own ears, I no longer know who I'm trying to convince. Still, they look at me, waiting.

"I think the Bible's a very human book." They grab and sip from their thin glasses, somehow never losing their focus on me. "I mean, the whole damn history of Israel is like a metaphor for the imperfections and moments of clarity that make up existence. God promises them something good; at first they listen, then their vision blurs, and they start looking for a life with more immediate gratification. Things start to suck for them, and they repent and begin the process over again. Look at King Solomon; God blesses him with incomparable wealth because he only asked for wisdom. Then, he becomes a miser and womanizer at the end of his life. And yet, the New Testament lists him as one of the heroes of the faith. I don't know. I guess I just think God knows I'm going to fail, but it feels like he doesn't want me to focus on that stuff that clouds our vision all the time."

They don't ask me to pray for them, they don't pass out and have holy visions—they just keep sitting there. I'm completely embarrassed at this point. Do I expect them to thank me, throwing their hands up and asking for WWJD bracelets? My school made me rehearse for this moment my whole life, but I'm fixated on their empty glasses, and how the insides are crusted with a honeycomb of dried foam, fossilized on their way to being emptied. I feel compelled to buy another round. Rob stops me, lifting at the knees and waving his palm in my direction, mouthing, *Stay there, stay there.* His other hand collects the glasses, smudging the foam with his pinched fingertips as all three collide, rattle, and come to rest.

[**Night** *is a pool collecting in the depressions of your cellar floor, the smell of musk and must concentrating each day. The bacteria grows in population, the new overtake the old, replacing histories, blurring the line between what is saved and who is doing the saving. You have sworn to save everything, thinking that if you hold it all in boxes in the basement, your heritage will not end with you.*

But isn't it silly that you tell yourself not to forget tragedies of the past? Do you want me to repeat myself? *history asks. It is as if by keeping a record of specific deaths, you'll at least be able to control how your end will descend.* "At least it won't be like that," *you might think.*

In the end, perhaps it would be better to forget for a day, a minute, forever, that endings are a whirlpool, a spinning roulette whose numbers have gone invisible.]

9

Seven Floods

1

My father, Alfred Parys, is flying over the tip of Cape Cod in 1963. He is fourteen. The curve of the earth is visible, cutting a graying arc into the sky. The land below him is an archipelago of winter white held in the open palm of the Atlantic. The view from the plane is oddly house-like, the window squared and large—not the stunted monocle of a 747 coach-class window. It is as if he were sitting on a couch in a living room, gazing upon the tundra surface of a backyard moon. Alfred soars, a camera in his hands. With the peephole pressed against the ridge of his eye socket, he searches for just the right moment to click the button, open the aperture, and stop this bit of motion forever. I don't know his destination, but I like to think that neither of us—me now, him then—cares about that part.

Around any photograph is negative space—a clearly marked set of borders that delineate where the picture ends and the not-picture shoots off into an eternity. No matter how many times I cradle the image, flipping the frame around instinctively to run my finger around the torn cardboard backing—ripped through as if someone had hoped to find something hidden in the air space—I always hold on to the idea that there's more to uncover. Every photograph is a reminder of the infinite unknown, and yet I keep whole books of them around to finger through, hoping that recalling the limits of what I already know will, one of these times, help me forget about just how much emptiness surrounds every image.

Turning the picture back to the front, I stare at the middle, working my way to the browned edge of the photo paper, and then finally the faded white frame. Eventually, my eyes have to leave the picture and reenter the space outside of it—back to me standing there and gently placing the 3" x 3" image on the bookshelf. The thing itself is not important, or at least, Alfred did not intend it to be anything beyond the miraculous thrill of seeing the world from the sky and then capturing a visual fragment of that experience. The photo was a photo until he died, when all of a sudden it became another in a long line of unanswerable questions. It is that idea, those questions—not the picture—I can't let go of, but since I can't hold an idea, I cling to the object.

2

There are piles of bulging, multi-subject notebooks everywhere. Whenever I move on, I leave behind spiral-bound, inky detritus. Rather than abandoning them, I am trying to create an investigable grid of my gleanings. Since Natalie and I got married during my senior year of college, my mother has been trying to motivate me to "go through" my "stuff."

"I want to turn your room into the 'red, white, and blue room,'" she tells me, on a recent patriotic kick.

"I'll do it over Thanksgiving," I say, and then say again every year. "I'll have more time then." But I don't. Instead, while everyone is still spooning the last of can-shaped cranberry sauce into pools of Gerber-ish squash, I sneak upstairs to avoid doing dishes. My room is being taken over by hand-held American flags, Uncle Sam dolls, a faux-antique door sign that reads "Home of the Brave" in a *Better Homes & Gardens*-style font. But there are remnants. Though she has taken down my Beatles and Oasis posters, sporty posters of Jose Canseco and David Robinson I've had since middle school are still tacked to the wall like a half-finished round of Minesweeper (a game I've always heard as *Mindsweeper*). "Remember before you got all artsy?" they ask, and it seems as if my mother is trying to recreate the past in an effort to preserve my history. If she is, the things that are visibly saved tell a misleading story.

The more present I become standing on the marble green carpet, the more aware I am that I have left many of these pieces intact, un-dusted—turning the assemblage of my room into a visual biography.

Artifact I:

A kiwi-strawberry Snapple bottle with a faded pink label—one of many. It is the first flavor I ever try, and I love it so much it leads me to think, "I should start a bottle collection." So, instead of throwing it away, I place it on the top of my bookshelf, flush left as if I am starting a sentence. Every time I try a different flavor, I rinse it and stamp it on a shelf until I have a dense paragraph. It occurs to me late in the collection process that the labels—Lemonade, Pink Lemonade, Iced Tea, Raspberry Lime Rickey—may be different, but the bottles themselves are the same: empty. I wonder if I'm saying anything at all, or if these are just rows of synonyms in search of a word that means: was once full, but is now empty.

Artifact II:

At the bottom of the closet there is a thin, maroon sleeping bag, crammed on the floor like a newspaper in a rusty birdcage. I lift a slippery fold and see an empty Tums container—citrus fruit flavors, extra calcium. When Cassy dumps me in eleventh grade I lay this sleeping bag across the bottom of the closet and climb in, holding the bottle of antacids and a white cordless phone. The closet is not wide enough for me to extend my legs, so I curl up sideways, my left hip pressing against the baseboard. I knew from TV that being dumped is something that leads people to take drugs, so I pop open the Tums and begin chewing the chalky tablets one by one. I want to eat the whole bottle so I have a reason to call her and say, "You see what you've done to me? I just ate eighteen Tums in half an hour!" I hold the phone, about to dial when my stepdad walks in and says, "Hey bud, Mom needs to make a call." I relinquish the phone. He sees the empty bottle in my other hand, and the whitish-orange dust lining my lips. "Heartburn?" he asks.

Artifact III:

I sit at the dark wood corner desk. Under a pile of papers I find the first chapter and hand-drawn map from *The Dagger of Lentura*—a fantasy novel I started in sixth grade after reading Terry Brooks's *The Sword of Shannara*. I had thought that by replacing the nouns, I could create a fantasy about how saving objects would eventually lead to saving people.

Artifact IV:

Above the drafts are two small drawers, one filled to bursting with notes, mostly from girls saying that they don't like me "like that." The one that is creased the most from unfolding-reading-folding is from Ruth, given to me in sixth grade:

> Bryan,
>
> *Let's just go back to being friends like we were before.*
>
> —*Ruth*

The next day our class has a Christmas party and someone brings a two-liter bottle of 7 Up. Seeing Ruth nearby, I fake a violent limp, grab the bottle, and begin chugging it, ignoring the choking sensation caused by taking so much liquid in at once. "This oughta make her feel bad about what she did to me," I think as the bottle drains and drains.

3

My sister is pissed, and the rain is pissing down in flowing walls that skid over the parking lot across the street from our house. She is raving and stomping around the kitchen, then the dining room.

My mother is on the phone with Betty, a woman from our church. "Flooded? The whole thing?" she says, sounding angry, but it is actually fear that has pitched her tone.

Betty's basement in Moultonborough, about an hour from our home in Laconia, is filling fast, soaking and swelling all the things they want to forget about, but feel they shouldn't. Things that are worth saving, but not using. In twenty years, what survives from their basement could be discovered by subsequent generations, and the words they will use for these sloughed off, semi-biographical debris will be *antique, heritage.*

But theirs is not the only heritage that is at risk of being walked off the plank during the storm. Years ago, after Alfred had died and my mother was forced to finally reckon with his cramped closet of clothes, Betty offered to bag them up, to take them off her hands and make a patchwork quilt out of his old flannels, pajamas, corduroys, and T-shirts.

"That would make a great gift for Allyson when she graduates high school," my mother tells her, relieved of the task of what to discard and what to anthologize.

But in the trash bags, they still sit, bundled and tied with half-knots, exhumed from a familiar darkness to a deeper, stranger one. *I'll get to it, I'll get to it,* Betty must think. But she is busy preserving her own heritage, however she defines that process, and the musky weight of the Parys patriarch is not high on her list of priorities.

And who can blame her? Where my sister sees the blue, paisley pajamas my dad wore almost nonstop in his last month, Betty sees pajamas. But what if she could sense the weight? What if everyone could decipher the code of extrafamilial effluvia, baldly sensing the gravity of each aged object? Every thrift store and flea market would moan with the mouths of hell and heaven, screaming their stories to the wealthy couples that peruse their aisles as they ask questions like, "Where's the Pyrex?" or "Do you have anything nautical?" Would they eat their dinners on a table if they knew where every one of its scratches came from—a child's fork dragged in protest of tonight's tripe, a dented leg from when the missus discovered there was a secret miss, so she kicked it, stubbing her toe as she demanded a divorce? The cacophonous yarns would be too long and complicated, their truths stretched from years of finding new ways to say *keep me and you'll know where you came from*; the pieces so deep and thick with layers that expiration dates and time-of-deaths would only add to the swirled patina of existence.

But now there is water, and everything is at stake.

So Allyson is frantic, begging someone to make the almost-hour's drive—easily doubled by the flash flooding of rain and night—to Betty's and rescue the bags that are already starting to bloat and draw the colors out of history. Without much thinking, my stepdad agrees and they hop in the minivan.

When they return, hugging darkened damp lumps, we find that 75 percent of the wardrobe had already been lost to mold, silenced by the slow rot that had been developing during those *I'll get to it* years, and polished off by a few hours of pooling.

4

I do not like new things. There are still gifts from my wedding that I have not used—a slow cooker, a Teflon-coated roasting pan, a microwave—and remain in my in-laws' basement. It is not that I do not want to use these items, though I couldn't care less for anything coated in Teflon, but rather it is because, unused, they are not mine. In order for a gift to actualize itself, one must open it and use it, saying to the giver, "This was yours, but you have given it to me, and its function has affected my life." If I don't use it, it never becomes something that is in danger of being damaged or left behind by its owner. I won't have to worry about saving it. It will root itself in independence, never thinking that those around it could leave, could die. Still in its original box, the slow cooker is autonomous—existence merely the warm, slow burn of time. It will never do what it was created to do, but in the same way, it will never run the risk of failing in its attempts.

In the book of Matthew, Jesus instructs, "Do not store up for yourselves treasures on earth, where moth and rust destroy," suggesting that there is a kind of mortal danger in the keeping of things: if you spend too much time saving things, there won't be any time left to save yourself. Later, he says, "where your treasure is, there your heart will be also."

My heart, it seems, is a closet populated with clothes from Goodwill and Salvation Army. The items are already half dead; the expectation of perfection is absent. I collect and save them from their mothball prisons. As a result, my outfits become a collage of history. But am I actually making things worse by taking the used-to-be treasures of others, the things they learned to part with, and making them my own?

One of my favorite salvaged T-shirts is light blue, thin like a second skin, and its center shows a graphic rendering of an old touch-tone phone being cracked in half by a wooden gavel that reads "Supreme Court" on the handle. The shirt is a relic, chronicling the court's decision that AT&T had become a monopoly and needed to diversify. They had stored up too much treasure. The names of all the subsequent companies that formed all across America as a result of the split were written on the front of the shirt, and included, among others: Pacific Telephone, Mountain Bell, Southern Bell, Bell of Pennsylvania, New England Telephone. Encircling the entire image, in quotes, is written: "Breaking Up Is Hard To Do!" I wear this shirt almost everyday after Cassy dumps me, and I wear it just as frequently when Natalie goes through a "maybe I'm too young to be married" crisis.

There is a green T-shirt that I have only worn once. It looks brand new, my mother having special ordered it from a custom clothing facility that she found online. The cotton is stiff, and scratches my back as if it had been woven from nettles. On the left breast, it displays the official seal of Belknap College, a tiny college in the remote town of Centre Harbor, New Hampshire, that shut down in the 1980s. Alfred Parys, one of their psychology alumni, did not make it much longer.

Unlike the photograph Alfred took from a plane over Cape Cod in 1963, the shirt is not yet an artifact. It is a reproduction of the feeling of loss, and so to look at it calls up a facsimile of grief. Like a wax figure in a Madame Tussaud museum, the shirt was made to trick the viewer backwards into the memory of a once-experienced emotion while at the same time creating distance from the reality it represents. Such objects replace real processes of reflection, and actual grief, with a self-curated emotional tour.

Still, even though I do not like the fit or feel of the new Belknap College shirt, I will not get rid of it, out of the abstract hope that I can one day imbue it with meaning. So, I will pack it away into one of the giant, green-topped Rubbermaid bins that Natalie and I buy after we get married to help us float from one apartment to the next. The shirt will lie folded next to bound pages of rescued words overflowing with college notes on entropy, drafts of numb-tongued poetry that will never be revisited, a B+ essay on how Penelope Lively's *Moon Tiger* uses flashbacks to show that facing death will cause a person to endlessly replay fragments of the past, like an old cassette ribbon, snagged and spun into unthinkable knots.

5

By the end of my senior year at Gordon College, my notebooks for the semester have tripled in size. It is the spring of 2004, Natalie and I are packing up our first apartment, and she is placing one after another of my pregnant notebooks into one of the huge bins. She holds up one from my freshman year.

"Can I throw this out?" she asks, gently paraphrasing, *Do not store up treasures—especially when those treasures are not really treasures.*

"Why?"

"It's your biology notes from three years ago."

"But I don't remember half of what's in there. Who knows what I'll need to look up someday. Do you remember what mitosis is?"

"No."

"See! Here, give it to me. I'll look it up."

"Good grief."

"Ha! Look at this stuff! Here are my notes from the C. S. Lewis class I took. Whenever Dr. Aiken said something weird, I'd write it at the top of the page, so I'd always have it, just in case." I try not to show that the prospect of losing notebooks is making my hands shake.

"In case of what?"

"Here's one! 'Where the chickens of love come home to roost.'"

"What the heck does that mean?"

"I don't remember! It's probably in here somewhere," I say, scanning old notes on *The Great Divorce*, a book about a cosmic breakup, the difference between the celestially saved and the eternally lost.

"I don't really see why we need to keep so many of these," she says. "I always chuck mine out on the last day of class."

"But what if you get famous someday?"

"You think that if I get famous, someone's going to come pawing through my notes from Research Methods?"

"You never know—people can read meaning into anything."

6

Quotes from my senior year notebook I want someone to read meanings into:

From Biblical Narrative (Dr. Paul Borgman)

"Borgman this, Borgman that." –Dr. Borgman

"By avoiding eyes, I don't get called on as much." –me

"As soon as I say '*qua*' you know I'm saying something important—because it's Latin." –Dr. Borgman

"Will we see Judas in Heaven in the way that Charlie saw Slugworth in the Chocolate Factory?" –me

From Literary Criticism (Dr. Anne Ferguson)

"I thought she said 'the fishy cot' instead of 'the fish he caught.'" –me

"Today in two thousand and . . . what is it? Three?" –Dr. Ferguson

"The Dubliners . . . actually takes place in Chile." –Lauren Brown, sitting next to me

"I'm not making you be a queer critic." –Dr. Ferguson

"I'M DROWNING." –me

7

The morning after Natalie graduates from college in 2006, we are awoken by a knock on our bedroom door. Aaron and Mariah, a married couple we've been sharing a house with in Beverly, Massachusetts are on the other side. They yell in, "The basement's flooded."

For the past week, Boston's North Shore has been hit with one of the hardest spring rains in memory. Every night after work/school the four of us head down to the basement armed with buckets and push brooms hoping to redirect the brown water seeping through the cracks over to the sump pump. It's getting mustier every day, but we are keeping it contained and away from the back corner where we store plastic bins of things we don't use and can't throw away.

Due to the preceding day's graduation festivities, however, we shirked our brooming during the most biblically torrential part of the storm. After Aaron and Mariah's announcement the next morning, I put on some blue flannel pajama pants and run halfway down the steps to the basement to see how bad it is. The electric organ that my friend Tom has been storing down there is half-immersed, the wood paneling expanding and lifting off the base. Silverfish are splayed and dead along the ripples of the water. A Rubbermaid ark bobs over the water's surface, bumping into a soggy box holding a wok I know I will never consider clean enough to ever use.

"My notebooks!" I yell. I roll my pants up as high around my legs as possible and start wading through water that looks as if it could give me malaria just by sight. I put a foot in and the edges blur. "Holy Moses, that's freezing," I yelp and rip my foot out of the water. I eye the floating bin, so far across the room, and think twice about braving the expelled groundwater. It is leaning more to the side, the green lid cresting the murk. Again, I think of the notebooks inside, and all the old drafts of plays and poems folded within their pockets. They're no good, but maybe they'll give those after me more source material than my father left for me. Plus, all those notes from Physical Science! I don't remember anything about atomic theory! It's all in there—something about plum pudding, James Clerk Maxwell, my professor who wouldn't stop holding his ear when he talked, a quantum theory that left us saying: *Who can really know anything?*

I wade in up to my thighs.

The water is surgical, incisive, like waking up after having an appendix out and shivering because the sterile chill of the operating room has cut to one's core, the cold swirling around bone, soaking into tissue and abiding.

The muscles in my legs are tight and I can barely move, as the water rises a bit higher up my legs with every urgent step, the dirty frost spreading. The bin has all but capsized when I reach it, and water is seeping in slowly. I float the bin of artifacts back to the steps, docking it with Aaron's help on the first dry stair. My legs are striped with chilled patches of red and white, growing colder still before the gelatinous blood starts finding veins again and I wait for the numbness of salvation to subside.

Part Three: **Temple / Tomb**

[*A temple* is a body filled, but with what depends on how you monitor what is going in, what enters through the double doors of a cracked rib cage. If the pews are scorched with ulcers, then your altar is a burning heart, and your chest is gurgling with the desire to keep its contents from being expelled. When Jesus walked into the temple at Jerusalem he did not find the showbread—the bread of presence—loaves required by God to be ready for his consumption at all times. Instead he found salesmen, and he turned over their tables. He threw them up, threw them out into the street saying that they'd turned not only his Father's house, but, through metaphor, his body, into a "den of thieves." Your father's house will become your body: don't let it be robbed.]

10

What Is in the Filling

I am counting back from one hundred, and then I'm out.

While I'm gone, the doctor at Lakes Region General in Laconia, New Hampshire, sticks a tuberous camera down my throat to search for why, at seventeen, I can't eat anything without burping up acid. Having seen this symptom in my father before he was diagnosed, my mother didn't waste time with Tums; she drove me straight to the hospital. Dr. Shafique tells me to swallow the camera, and I oblige immediately, even though my conscious mind is buried under strata of sleep. We sleep, and we remember to breathe—I get this. But to physically respond to language without being *there* is another thing entirely. Breathing is muscle memory—our bodies remember. I do not know this doctor personally, nor have I ever practiced chugging imaging machinery, so my throat can't call this one up from the past and simply duplicate it. This is deep-seated obedience—I will do what I'm told whether my mind knows it or not.

So, would I swallow a camera if God asked me to?

The first two words that I learn to spell that are not *cat*, *dog*, or *God* are *stop* and *obedience*. Obedience comes via a song we repeat daily as a class in kindergarten at Laconia Christian School: "O-B-E-D-I-E-N-C-E / Obedience is / the very best way / to show that you believe." Stop. Obey. From the beginning, I ingest the idea that to stop obeying is to stop believing.

I can't seem to obey anything without extending the act of obedience into some kind of belief. Would I make a cheese omelet if Dr. Shafique asked me to? Would I promise to follow him all of my days, if he asked, believing he could offer an afterlife that fulfills the empty person I supposedly am without someone to believe in?

I wake up in the recovery room in different clothes, and my mother is reading a magazine next to me. "They think it's esophagitis." She thumbs the pages, but her head has stopped following the shuffle. She tilts her head slightly and her eyes tighten and bend around her last word, searching for why it feels so familiar. Her mouth opens, then closes, then: "They say you're not chewing enough."

Communion at Laconia Christian Fellowship is more informal than the Catholic Eucharist, or the monthly Communions of Presbyterian and other mainline Evangelical denominations—even beyond the fact that we meet in a high school gymnasium. We hold our version every Sunday—a weekly reminder to look inside and find the gaps of our soul we've not allowed Christ's blood to fill. Those who serve Communion are not required to be clergy. Before we are to receive "the elements" of Communion, a man at the front of the church says into the microphone, "If God has laid it upon your heart to serve Communion this morning, please go and prepare the elements."

Those who feel led—a word used to test one's level of obedience—walk quietly over the plastic-tiled gym floor to a pine altar in the back of the sanctuary. On top of the altar is a velvet runner that hangs over each side. Resting on the cloth are six plastic platters, three of which hold a dusty pile of crumbled matzo crackers, and three arranged with rows of thimble-sized cups that have been filled with white grape juice from an eye dropper—symbolic trays of the body and blood of Jesus. Each volunteer cradles a plate and steps—lightly to avoid the suggestion of blood spilling—to the front of the congregation, turns, and waits for the final instructional inquiry: "Won't you come and receive the elements?"

The white Communion elements at LCF weren't always this monochromatic. When my family first started attending when I was in seventh grade, the "body" took the form of loaves of bread lovingly baked by Mrs. Shoemaker, whose reputation for rolls and cinnamon buns was known in homes and restaurants throughout Belknap County. In the Catholic and Episcopal traditions, the blood is in the form of wine. For reasons I was never sure of, we substituted red grape juice for the more traditional wine, perhaps partly due to cost, but also because the only context for hearing the word "alcohol" at church was in reference to addiction. I'm guessing that combining the solution of Christ with the problem of alcoholism mixed the metaphor for them. Taking the visual reference even further from Christ's blood, the church eventually switched to white grape juice due, perhaps, to an influx of children spilling their symbols all over their Sunday best.

The loaves that Mrs. Shoemaker used to bring to church would sit against the wall on the altar, causing bowed heads to turn. When communion came, the bread was ripped in half and placed on the platters. The tan arc of the risen loaf was like the skin of the risen Lord—not burnt and death-bound, but filled with celestial warmth. Each torn section looked hearty, yet airy; filling, but not in the way the word is used at family reunions in reference to someone's fudge. In essence, the loaves were transcendent—containing physical substance, but suggestive of the fact that there is more to fill than just the stomach.

Once the servers had positioned themselves at the front of the church, congregants would then tear off a small piece before grabbing a tablespoon-sized cup of grape juice. As was custom, we would bring the elements back to our folding chairs, wait for a short blessing, then partake—morsel of bread first, then drip of juice.

I am twelve when we first start attending LCF, and during one of the first Communion services, I look over the crowd and spot a beaming, hungry face among them, his dark hair pushed to the side and glued to the edge of his face with the faint sheen of sweat. "Please, take and eat," says a voice from the pulpit. I watch as the smiling man's hand—bursting with a fistful portion of the bread—rises up to his mouth, the mound of bread like a sponge he will use to scrub his spirit shiny. The rest of us have long since swallowed, and the pulpit voice tells us, "Take the cup and drink." I sip without taking my eyes off this glutton for forgiveness, and the liquid goes down the wrong pipe. I choke and lurch forward a little, trying to keep from making a scene.

I lean over to Mom and whisper for a piece of Trident. She starts pawing with her Revlon nails through a black-and-white–checked purse, a dozen bracelets clanging on each wrist. My chest bubbles with acid, and the blood of Christ burns all the way down. "I don't think I have any left," she whispers back. "Ask Dad and see if he has any Breath Savers."

I am distracted by a sudden commotion over by the altar. The picked-over bread is sitting like a carcass, and a swarm of children, no older than eight, are circling the altar—snotty, sweaty hands grabbing at the loaves and gnawing at it by the palmful.

In 1 Corinthians 11, the Apostle Paul addresses the digestive issues the church in Corinth is having with Communion. Because Christ meant for Communion to be modeled after Passover—another time where blood saved people from death—the Corinthian Communion was probably more of a feast and certainly not comprised of Styrofoam-like discs and diminutive plastic cups. It seemed that people were showing up at church treating the Lord's Supper like it was a Chinese buffet. The food was gone and people were drunk before others even had a chance to partake. Paul reminded them that this wasn't a holy pub, and, for Christ's sake, have a snack before church if you're that ravenous.

I'm starving.

"Ma, where can I put the peanut butter fudge?" I ask, having just arrived at a family reunion in the fall of 2008. I am twenty-five, we are at Aunt Becca's place, and this is the first reunion of this scale in over a decade. I am here as part of the Dame branch of the Swain family. It is an unseasonably balmy September day, and the edges of the fudge are already bending slightly, the fat from the butter warming and glistening like the ridge of sweat forming on my brow, like squares of skin losing hold of a summer tan.

"Here, just put it next to Don's apple crisp," she says, moving Aunt Linda's corn flake treats over a bit to make room. I set down the aluminum pan filled with the fudge I made that morning, knowing full well that, now that I'm an adult and expected to bring food to these occasions, they will most likely remember me less by what I say and more by what I bring to the table. After a quick hug of hello, my mother's face takes on a somber glance as she points to the dessert and says, "That's Aunt June's carrot cake."

"Oh, well I wouldn't expect any less," I say, nodding a hello at the cream cheese frosting. Aunt June died in 1987—the same year as Alfred—but her carrot cake is broken and eaten in remembrance of her every time we meet.

She had always organized the gatherings, and it was her dying wish that we continue the tradition after she had departed. Even though it is my mom's sister Linda—whose crispy-sweet corn flake balls are already famous—who made the cake this time, she wouldn't dare call it her own.

"I know, it's supposed to have nuts in it, but Todd and Tommy don't like nuts," Aunt Linda says as she scurries over.

"That's fine," I say. "I wouldn't mind either way."

"You like nuts?" she asks in a pitch that increases and peaks in falsetto by the end of the last syllable. "Oh *dahn* it."

She speaks with that mid-New Hampshire accent that all five of the Dame sisters comfortably reside in. The most notable pronunciation is of my mother's name—Barbara Ray—that fluctuates from Bahb, to Bobbie Ray, to its most cozy-tongued, Bah-Ray.

She turns to Mom, crestfallen, "Bahb, you should've told me he liked nuts."

"No, really. It's not a big deal," I say. "Look, did you see I made fudge?"

"*You* made this?" she asks in surprise. "It looks so filling; I really shouldn't," she continues, reaching for a bent cube.

By high school, I start getting heartburn from Communion almost every week. And while our church places only a symbolic lens on the bread and juice as the body and blood, rather than the Catholic view of transubstantiation, I can't help but think that choking on symbols of my Savior is not a good sign for the state of my immortal soul.

It starts with the body getting stuck in my teeth. "Take and eat," the pastor says, and we all pop the cracker crumbs into our mouths. Mine gets lodged in a back molar, and I frantically use my tongue to fish out the lodged Messiah. All at once, the pulpy mash springs from its dental crevice and shoots down my throat. I give a quiet *hrmph* as the pastor continues reading from Scripture, "This is my blood poured out for you. Take and drink." I sip and feel the juice sink into the gritty mess in my throat, the tablespoonful only enough to make a thick, holy slurry. When the blockage gives, it goes down hard, and finishes with a liquid burp. I cannot keep it all down, as much as I obey the directions, and with all this symbolism of blood saving blood, life needing to ingest death, I wonder why it is harder to keep it down than it is to cough it up.

X

The story of my aunts, the Dame sisters, is comprised of disappearances that leave everyone hungry. Their mother Sally—"Nanny" to her thirteen grandchildren—governs them. She recently celebrated her eightieth birthday, despite leukemia that keeps rising up and then receding just as death decides we've been adequately reminded of what's coming. Over the last few years her health and mobility have deteriorated to the point where she can no longer live on her own. When it recently came time to move to an assisted living apartment building her stubborn wit fights it with a fiery independence she had gained decades prior when her husband, Ed, left her and moved to Arizona. Late in his life, afflicted with a severe case of emphysema due to the amount of smoke he chose to fill his lungs with, he returned, long after Nanny had finished raising the five girls.

Ed Dame. When Ed left, he left the Dames—setting a standard of male absence. Each daughter has lost a spouse to either divorce or, in my mother's case, an early death. The symbol of patriarchal emptiness that Ed embodied in his absence was perpetuated in his return by the tracheotomy that rendered him mute. He would reappear only to have his voice leak out of his throat and abandon everyone, leaving us with his ghostly presence in aviator sunglasses, a short-sleeved checkered shirt, and a peppery, trapezoidal buzz cut—a VFW puppet king. Before he became completely bedridden, Ed would drive his Buick to our house, park in the driveway, and honk, since he could no longer make it up the brick steps that led to our greying house.

"Grampa's here," my mom would yell from the kitchen, her left hand covering the mouthpiece of the phone. "Go out and say hi."

I would do so reluctantly, approaching the open passenger-side window, too nervous to move to the driver's side. He would then pick up his white, electric speech aid and hold it to the flattened-penny–sized hole in his throat.

"Ee-er auw ohr, ote."

"Hi grampa."

"Kerr awch ehn verrecht."

"I'm gonna go get Mom," I say, sprinting back into the house, the echo of his cramped language sounding like symbols, not words.

When Ed dies, he leaves behind the five Dame girls and their thirteen combined children, all of whom, with the exception of my sister Allyson, are male. It makes sense then that it is the matriarchal symbol of Aunt June's baking that brings the relatives together again and again.

The gastronomy of family get-togethers is dominated by what we've come to call *pickies*—a school of snacking that renders the idea of a main dish useless. Holiday turkeys and hams are forked at right out of the oven, despite the constant cluckings of: "Oh, I shouldn't . . ." "Don't tell, ok?" and "Alright; one more, one more."

Right around the time that Ed passed away, the snacking started taking a low-calorie turn. Death caused an obsession with weight control that trickled off the platters of family holidays and into our quotidian pantries. Butter became margarine, and then something that is two churns away from the plastic tub it comes in. Eggs were bought in pourable form and turkey was paraded out as bacon, hot dogs, and burgers. We started eating devil's food cookies redeemed and sucked dry by the chemical flavorings of Snackwell's. We bought boxes of treats from a company calling itself Guilt-less Gourmet.

We looked for and were offered a substitute, a savior—an intermediary that appeared to fill a human need, without any of the calories. But it was a dupe. The food was processed beyond salvation, becoming only a representative of the name we give it. Not so much a symbol, but a slow bout of bait and switch to convince us that if these food-facades contained enough artificial fillers, we wouldn't be able to realize that the filling is fake.

Because the congregation is failing to recognize the layers of meaning in Communion, Paul tells them in 1 Corinthians 11:30 (NIV) that this "is why many among you are weak and sick, and a number of you have fallen asleep." Does he mean that they get so off-their-heads wasted that they pass out? Or, is there more symbolism here, and it is that their souls have been drugged into a state in which only their bodies are obedient to what is going on?

I have trouble sleeping because of the heartburn. I lie on my back and the acid slushes back and forth, leaping in spikes of full-chest-cavity hiccups. I'm thinking about why my ex-girlfriend, Lizzy, never wanted to kiss me, and about why I'm thinking about Lizzy at night and not praying much. I'm thinking about how my father had esophagitis before he was diagnosed with cancer of the esophagus, that his father died well before I was born, and that my mom's father smoked himself voiceless then died before I'd reached double digits.

But still I eat hot peppers straight from the jar. Sometimes, when they are gone, I lift the glass lip to my mouth and drink the spicy vinegar, feeling it open my eyes as it hits my throat and starts to burn and foam.

Do I not care about longevity? That you aren't what you eat, but that what is eating you determines whether or not you keep a walking pace towards death, or are jolted into a full-on sprint? There will be no time to make a heritage, no time to make it to thirty-eight and then to thirty-nine—a simple continuation of life the preceding generations of males in your family could not accomplish.

Long ago, it seems, I replaced reality with symbols; for a symbol is not the thing itself, it is only a container. Just as you can't judge a book by its cover, you can't know what's inside something simply from the symbols that contain it, as if touching a box of crackers meant you were eating what was inside. Similarly, if I take Communion, then am I obedient to God? Or, if I could get Lizzy to kiss me, would it mean I have broken my solipsism, connected with another human, and at least flirted with the attempt to continue life?

Another translation of Paul's warning in verse thirty: "That is why many of you are weak and sick and some have even died."

To fall asleep is to die; please, let me stay an insomniac for a while longer.

All that I have left are symbols. My father dies and is resurrected in photographs as a two-dimensional image of what I could be like, and so I hold on to photos in hopes of exposing the eternity behind death. When I get glasses in middle school, my aunts, mother, and older sister Allyson say, "You look just like him," then crane their necks at the images my face conjures. When I am in college, Allyson visits me after I have my appendix out, and I look over at her slowly. She sees me, unshaven, in a blue-checkered johnny and fed through an IV, and immediately walks out and cries. I look like death, but not everyone's death. I look like her, our death. Death is a thin cotton robe that can't cover your ass. Death that works intravenously, fed into our bodies without us ever needing to open our mouths to accept it.

"You just look so much like him, sorry," she says when she comes back in.

Perhaps it is not that I'm obsessed with symbols, but that symbols are obsessed with death. Lizzy wouldn't kiss me. A kiss is a step forward towards sex, life, two people agreeing that if we must die, let's do it together and leave something behind for others to read into. For me, the kiss of death is not being kissed. Even though one of my aunts watched a father who would've smoked through his tracheotomy hole, she still smokes, still sneaks outside in the snow at Christmas parties to light up and kiss death. She has two kids, she's been kissed at least twice, so what's the big deal, I guess.

Like a sentient cancer, Judas kisses Christ, and then they arrest Christ and sentence him to death. This is after the Last Supper where Jesus breaks bread and pours wine, saying of both, "This is me," and no one, the meat-heads, gets the symbolism. The disciples weren't reading into anything. But then looking back, they got it, and they must've hated themselves. Judas buys land with history's heaviest blood money, and then eviscerates himself, his intestines poured out over the land. He killed himself with a kiss too.

So now we take Communion, "in remembrance of him," and seem to be saying each time, "We get it now, O God, why were we so stupid?"

Aunt Becca is rattling my mom's arm, "Bah-Ray, come and read your poem for everyone." She turns her head to the picnicking crowd, her thin hairs twitching as she yells, "Everyone! Bobbie's got a poem she wants to read. Get over here and form a circle around Nanny and Aunt Peg!"

"I don't need to read it," Mom says to Becca. "I put copies of it on the tables anyway." It is a poem that, though she didn't mean it to be, is about how death shatters a family and then forms a new shell around the vacuity. Now she gets its mortal weight, but the knowledge is of no use; Becca has made up her mind. In the hot sunlight, Mom reluctantly walks over to where Nanny is sitting in a collapsible nylon chair, her bad leg raised on a small table in front of her, a Chinet plate of unfinished potato salad resting next to the air-casted foot. Nanny's sister, Peg, sits to her right, her hands and head shaking due to an aggressive case of Parkinson's disease. The impetus for this particular reunion is, in part, Nanny and Peg's poor health, their names soon to be added to the poem's list of lives turned symbolic.

117

The reading begins, and Mom only has to mention a few key names of relatives long or recently expired before the weeping begins. Though the poem is in the lilty ababcdcd format common to mom's greeting card poetry, it's clear the syrupy structure contains more elegy than celebration. The name "Aunt June" is mouthed—"Then, in 1986, cancer crept in"—and without taking her eyes off the page, she sees and grabs Nanny's outstretched hand. As if it had been waiting for the lead-in to Aunt June's story, a cell phone rings in a boogie beat at full volume. I recognize it as the tone I've tried to get Mom to change on numerous occasions. The hiccupping sobs now blend with the 8-bit symphony from her pocket—the wailings of aunts and microchips harmonizing.

Amidst the pats on the back surrounding my mother, I sidle over to the dessert table, trying to escape the awkward stew of emotions and missed calls. I stare at the glistening root cake, a couple squares sliced out of one end, the edges rounded and blurred by the fingernails of a picking aunt. I cut a cube with a purple plastic knife and rest the piece on a cocktail napkin, orange oil seeping through the first two folds. I take and eat—the cool frosting slides up behind the back of my front teeth and coats the roof of my mouth while a delicate suspension of carrot, flour, and overturned death crumbles on to my tongue. Aunt Sandra approaches me in earnest: "You know that's Aunt June's carrot cake, don't you?"

"Mmhmm," I say, letting the bite swirl into my insides. "Did you try my fudge?"

If tiny things point to the big ending, then I will make peanut butter fudge, flesh-colored with bone-white chunks of peanuts and dermal butter, and, probably, specks of my dead skin sprinkling in while I mix the elements with a wooden spoon. I will create a solid body, which I can then pierce and divide up amongst those who are still living, my peripheral past, my symbols of the future. It will be delicious, and people will roll their eyes and moan as they kiss it, even though it is too filling, and even though there is not as much powdered sugar as there should be because I ran out halfway through, and my wife said, "It'll be fine. It's just fudge."

No, it isn't.

[*A tomb reflects emptiness—even though it can be stuffed full of tattered, wasted things—reminding you that you tried to fix them over and over, but in the end, they were broken and they broke you. The idea was to have an idea; then, after much lip-licking and rolling back your eyes to lock your vision with the brain, with where the idea originated, you put your hands to work. But there is no light, no life in a tomb even when you descend concrete stairs and populate it for a moment. You are a guideless visitor, kicking up dust that makes you back up, waving your hands, saying* "I give up, ok, I'm outta here."]

11

Breaking a Light Bulb

1

"If Yan can cook, so can you," I mouth along with the mid-90s cooking show pioneer, Martin Yan, mimicking his two-dimensional movements. I am thirteen, and I watch way too much TV. His knife skills are perfectly buoyant: holding a purple onion with his knuckles folded inward, severing mathematical cubes. He doesn't even look at what he's doing, but rather he looks at the camera with a smile so intense it forces his eyes shut and rocks his head from side to side. I look back at him, cubing the air with the remote, using the arm of a flaking leather chair as a chopping block and thinking, *hey, I could do that*. Staring with my mouth stuck so open that it is on the verge of drooling, I feel the plastic edge push against my hand, slicing my left index clean off. *That would've been it*, I think, and almost see a phantom finger dangling from its final ligament.

2

My mother is sick in bed under a spell of vertigo, two pillows propping up her head. She calls out my name with a fragility that I just barely hear over a rerun of some sitcom. I run in to see her, asking "What?" in a tone that mimics her own. With an arm folded over her eyes and her face as yellow as a fluorescent bulb, she mutters, "Can you cut up the steak for dinner before Dad gets home?"

"Really?" I say. "You'll let me use the big knife?

"Yes. Be—" she pauses for a second to catch up with the speed of speech, "—very careful."

I wait until I've paced out of her room before I start running towards the kitchen, past the den where Caleb is playing *Earthworm Jim 2* on our Sega Genesis.

"I get to cut the meat!" I yell to him, throwing a fist in the air.

"What? Great. Whatever," he says in a slack monotone, his unblinking eyelids not moving from the screen. After I've made it into the kitchen and begin my search for the knife, I hear a thud of plastic hit the thin den carpet. "Well that's just great," he screams, "you just made me die!"

I ignore him and scan the small crock on the counter that holds spatulas, wooden spoons, and old knives. Each handle sticks out of the mass like a cluster of question marks, so I tug at random, trying to find the right one. The first comes up a peeler, the next a potato masher. I pull a curved, black handle, and the blade is shiny but more squared than the chef's knives I've seen on TV. It is so dull that, running a pinch of fingertip along the edge, I can't quite tell which is the sharpened side.

Using the tip, I drag the knife through the plastic film that covers the two pounds of London broil, the red juice spilling onto the cutting board, then dripping over the edge and down the front of our dark wooden cabinets. I drop the knife and rip two squares of Bounty from the dowel suspended over the sink just quickly enough to ensure the blood doesn't make it to the floor.

I wash my hands thoroughly, as I've seen Martin Yan and Julia Child do on PBS, then slap a floppy slab of meat onto the counter with my left hand. I bring the knife down slowly along a white membrane, thinking it a natural spot to begin segmentation. When I start sawing, nothing happens. The meat is so elastic and the blade so worn that it seems I'm not doing anything but giving the beef a localized massage.

I pick the raw meat up and, holding it firmly in my left fist, bend the steak over the edge of the blade. I figure I can get more leverage if I just push the knife up through, as if I'm sewing a button. But as the tip breaks through sinew, the force of my arm speeds the blade up and across the inner base of my left index finger. I drop everything and stare at the mouth that has opened on my hand, seeing white dots in the blood that, for the moment, is motionless, as if the blood hasn't realized it has been given an escape route. I cannot figure out what the dots are, but the first thought is: *capillary.*

"I'm bleeding!" I yell to Caleb, not so much out of distress, but out of some awe-struck pride.

"Ah, it's probably just ketchup," he says back, his connection to the Sega remaining unbroken.

"No, I can see capillaries! They're floating all over the place. They look like ghosts!" With this, I grab rough handfuls of paper towels and wrap them around the wound, my blood soaking through each quilted pore and spreading across its surface like a topographical map. I run into the den, saying, "See!"

"Oh my *gawd*!" he says, dropping the controller. "Go show Mom!"

"But she's got vertigo. What if she throws up?"

"What else are you gonna do?"

I walk as calmly as possible into my mother's room. After I tell her, I'm surprised how little her demeanor changes; her mind is still trying to push its way out of a funnel cloud.

"Apply light pressure," she says, speaking like she is dealing with a patient at the private practice where she is a part-time surgical nurse. "But you'll have to wait until Dad gets home before anyone can take you anywhere."

"But that's not for another two hours!"

"Just apply pressure and hold it upright. If I drove now, that would just be a crazy idea."

3

"How long have you been watching that TV?" my mom asks, annoyed, as she emerges from the laundry room holding a warm womb of faded bath towels she has had since her first marriage.

"Only since *The Price Is Right*," I say, seeing time as defined by blocks of televised footage.

"Well, I think that's enough for one morning, don't you?" She shakes her head, trying to coax the right half of her wavy brown hair off her shoulder, but only a small section is flung back.

I stare, using my eyebrows to say, *No, Mother. TV doesn't just end.*

She returns my gaze, but her eyes become hazy in a familiar way. She is searching for something, anything for me to do other than watch more TV. I've done my Saturday morning chores, and my dad's not due back from work until lunch, so she will most likely settle on something insignificant, something that really doesn't need doing.

Her eye glaze clears, and her mouth opens gently into a pinched circle, leaking the words, "Could you—" Her head turns down to the left, that stubborn column of hair now falling over her cheek, "—bring this stuff back down to the basement for me?" She tightens her grip on the towels, then flips a wrist outward from the pile to point at a wiped-clean canning pot and a red-handled hammer that my dad has left leaning against the cellar door.

When I see the hammer, I see an invitation. I pick it up and my mind digs for a how-to of the item, landing on a scene from *Karate Kid*. Leverage—hold the hammer near the rear of the handle, swing, and the nail will immerse itself in splinters in one strike.

Getting to the basement requires a three-step process of illumination. The first comes after raking the heavy wooden door over the jaundiced shag carpet of our dining room with a resistant whoosh. Affixed to the upper right inside the doorway there is a large, bald light bulb with a short, metal-beaded pull chain. For some reason, the bulb's largeness doesn't make it any brighter than any other lamp in the house. Instead, its glow is barely enough to show the wallpaper it is mounted over—a collage of old *Mademoiselle* covers. Due to the pasting job, you can only guess the full name of the magazine, the only visible snippets being *Mademo, sell, demo*, printed beneath vintage photos of women that, in this light, look as much like cartoons as they do real people.

The naked bulb's faint glow reveals a small, round, black switch on the opposing wall at the top of the stairs. It is an old, sluggish switch, the snap not happening without just enough concerted effort that you notice it. When the switch finally gives, another unshaded bulb turns on, this time off in the distance to the right of the bottom of the stairs. Between the pull of light one and the snap of light two, the first and last stairs can be seen. But the middle remains thick, shadowy. There is a clear beginning and end, but to bridge the two, you have to go it blind.

I hang the hammer gently on the wall, and continue walking down to the base of the stairs, where there is just enough light to outline the dust-rounded corners of objects in the sloughed-off corners of the basement. The expectation of cobwebs is not unfounded. The whole expanse of half-fixed clocks and jagged piles of project scrap feels comatose, and thus somehow alive—the items weren't abandoned; they were just unintentionally never revisited.

Under the stairwell, where I place the large pot, is a canning cemetery. Some of the rusty-topped Mason jars sit empty, others still filled with zucchini relishes that were never used on charred burgers or tied with a ribbon and given out to church members last August. Centered in the middle of the basement, there is a pool table with a broken leg that has been that way since we moved in when I was three. It is piled high with wooden liquor crates and faded boxes that once concealed Christmas gifts—some of those presents now lying crookedly only a few feet away.

The third light is screwed in over the top of a workbench my father Alfred used in the brief period of health he had enjoyed between moving into this house and taking ill. Once at the workbench, I need to feel around the wall, making contact with the musty damp that shrouds the way. No matter how many times I come down here, I always have to go through this series of empty swipes and false starts before finally touching on a switch and flicking it. The light hesitates, a gap of skittish blackness between the current's first impulse and the bulb's yellowish, blinking reaction. The light buzzes, loud and ambient, an off-white noise that does anything but hang in the background.

Since my father's death in 1987, the tools have been left on the bench to preserve themselves, most of the dust remaining in place—a reminder of the passing of time. Each time I am down here I start in the middle of the bench and work my way left, running my eyes over the cracked 8-track of Janis Joplin's *The Pearl* and countless coffee tins that hold rusty screws, frayed wires, and other sundries that were put to use and laid to rest by the hands of one who understood them.

A homemade vise grip and hand-crank grinding wheel are affixed to the left end of the worktable. I put my hand in the vise and turn the crank, disturbing a small whorl of dust from its resting place. I tighten the vise, applying pressure in gradual increments until the blood thumps between my fingernail and bone. After releasing my hand, I grab the handle of the grindstone and spin it furiously until its low, buzzing pitch accelerates to a whirring squeal. I sometimes lay a nail against the wheel in order to see a spark, to generate my own electricity. I let go at the height of the wheel's speed and watch as it seems to spin faster without me for a couple moments, then slows as if realizing it is spinning just to spin.

The rest of the basement has no light fixtures at all, the only illumination coming by way of daylight, diffuse and gray through the decades-old cellar windows. Away from the windows and the humming light over the workbench, the farthest reaches of the basement remain completely black, concealing who knows what sorts of rotten projects too far gone to even daydream about resurrecting.

I move to the opposite end of the bench and pay my respects to the only still-actualized idea in the work area: a four-foot block of wood suspended on each end by old swing set chains attached to the moldy ceiling. Along each of the four long sides is glued a red Taster's Choice lid, and affixed to each lid is a corresponding jar filled with its own type of bolt, nut, or screw. If my father needed a dry-wall screw, he simply spun the piece of wood, jangling the metal maracas until he found the right jar, and unscrewed it from its fixed, rightful place. I get all kinds of ideas.

4

The light bulbs Natalie and I buy after we get married in 2003, when we are twenty and twenty-one respectively, are cheap, and they burn themselves out often before the end of a seasonal apartment lease. After a few years we spring for bulbs that shudder when you turn them on, as if they were waking up in the middle of the night to the ringing of a telephone. They are compact fluorescent bulbs (CFLs)—far more sustainable and efficient than any light I grew up underneath. Their light can last up to 10,000 hours; by the usage calculations printed on the box, that equals nine years of on-demand clarity for the consumer sitting in the dark.

I hesitated when I bought them, first because they are four times the price of a normal, incandescent bulb. But this is due mostly to my knee-jerk Yankee frugality, which kicks in every time I learn that something costs more than seven dollars. As I stood there staring at the rack, a grad school friend assured me that, of course, the math checks out—spend more now, get a heck of a lot more later.

But I still balk at the thought that this light could outlive me.

In nine years I will be thirty-six. When my dad was thirty-six, he had one year to go. Did he have to buy bulbs in that last year—did the house lamps go out before he did?

It scares me that over the next nine years, my life will be threatened exponentially more than this new bulb. When I'm driving, just feet away from speeding cars going in the opposite direction, the bulb will still be screwed into place, its coiled shape like a sleeping snake. Of course, there is the possibility of a power surge, or someone knocking the lamp over, but even in that case, the lamp's ceramic base would likely suffer more than its luminescent organ. It'll be there every day when I get home, unmoved, while I'll have dodged cars, flights of stairs, silent people that could be about to lose it, unpredictable vision blackouts about which medical professionals would later say, "There was just no way to predict this. To see it coming." No way to see it, except to think about it at night, after Natalie hits the lights, and the last flashes of cones and rods bury themselves in my skull, becoming the memory of light in a darkened world.

I want bulbs that fade fast, that shatter at the slightest provocation. I want, after only a few months time, to pull the chain and see its last gasp flash before my eyes in a near explosion of purity—its death ray brighter than any light that shone during its preceding pabulum of day-to-day illumination. Then, I want to replace it with another one, smiling because I'm still here.

5

Wires, like ideas, are a series of tentative connections. Though I re-research it every few months, I do not understand electricity. Saying the word conjures up scenes from old, educational Disney cartoons with crisscrossed lines of color following a grid. Benjamin Franklin and his kite and key are in animated Technicolor, and when lightning shoots down the string, his body convulses in an electrocuted spread eagle, his skeleton and outer appearance flashing back and forth.

When I look at a light bulb, I do not get any bright ideas. Instead, I see the ideas of others—impulses that came to them in a flash of logic. I see their illumined ability to translate the impulse into an orderly list, and then complete each itemized task patiently, one by one, thereby connecting the idea with reality.

Though I have bought dozens of bulbs, I have never personally bought a lamp. I own a few, but they were bestowed upon me, to make things easier: "Have some of our light," they remind me. Most of them were wedding gifts, and are desk lamps that light up corners, not rooms. In most apartments, I have two choices: the incomprehensibly blinding ceiling lights that are wired throughout each room, or the manageable lamps that make reading a book possible, but leave the rest of the room a dim mystery.

One of these desk lamps I am quite attached to. A pale, blue, frosted dome rests atop three thin metal arms joined to a pole at the center that runs down to a circular, weighted base, and casts a soft glow rather than a slicing brightness. When one of the arms breaks when we are living in our seventh apartment in less than five years, I pick up a hammer and a tiny nail and bend it around the joint where the arm meets the base. It wobbles slightly, but when I put the dome back on, everything locks into order—I think I have fixed it. Every time we move, I remove the dome and immediately the broken arm falls out of its sore socket.

We do eventually get one floor lamp. It is something I inherit from my office when I leave a web-editing job in 2007. A brushed steel, two-headed sleek piece from IKEA, it works miracles in lumens. A slider controls the large head—I can choose the level of illumination. The smaller head is connected to a foot switch; turning it on is as simple as taking a step towards the light.

Moving into apartment no. 8, we lose the large head to the pavement I was carrying it over. We keep it until no. 9, using the smaller head as a reading lamp for the bedroom. Before packing it however, my father-in-law and I make sure to disassemble the fixture and bulb so that it will not meet with the same fate. I take the clear, small bulb—incandescent because I was too cheap to look for the custom-size CFL—and pack it into the moving trailer, but soon forget where.

After unpacking most of the boxes, the light bulb is nowhere to be found, so the skeletal lamp stands uselessly in the corner of our bedroom. A couple mornings after moving in, I make Turkish coffee to go and grab my smallest travel mug out of the cupboard. I unscrew the lid and, from the tilted angle that I'm holding the cup at, notice a soap bubble has formed a dome in the middle of the cup. This wasn't rinsed well enough, I think, and I try to pop it with my finger and it goes *plink*. Bubbles should not *plink*. I stare at it longer and notice a tiny coiled filament inside the bubble and can make out copper threading near its base. Ah. *Here* is the light bulb. I try to dislodge it, but it barely budges. I try again, and it squeaks further down, into the thinnest part of the mug's hourglass shape. Now it's truly stuck. I see a knife in the sink—no, that's just asking for a bleeding retina, I say. Instead, I try wetting the edges of the bulb, hoping it will then slide out with ease.

It doesn't. I think about the knife again, but eventually settle on a small soup spoon. The utensil finds its way around the glass shell, lifting the lubricated shell ever so slightly. I pull back, not wanting to get overzealous. I try again. Though I am expecting it, I still pin my eyes shut in an arm-hair-raising flinch when the pressure builds and the bulb explodes in front of my face, barely missing my eyelids; I am still stunned by such a sudden release of trapped air.

[*A **temple** lies on either side of your forehead, and when you rub slow circles into each depression with a thumb or ring finger, it tells people that you have a headache. Paradoxically, the more pressure you apply to the divots, the less your head hurts—or the less you think about the pain as centralized in your head. What if it was all in your head? Or, what if none of it was, and the pain you feel is simply the result of realizing you're empty?*

Don't worry; this may not be a bad thing. There is a difference between emptying and emptiness, and as long as you keep moving, keep scooping and dumping the water out of the sinking birch canoe of your skull, you might actually get somewhere.]

12

In Exile

1

In the school gymnasium where our church is held every Sunday, there is an exposed, blue tarpaulin tube that runs up the backside of the gym and then across the inner peak of the ceiling. The brand name written on the side is Airmax, and this is how we refer to it, though I have no idea what it means. Intermittently throughout the service, the Airmax turns on, and hot, dry air churns in its motorized base, then explodes in heated bursts up through the tubing. The air stretches and tugs at the plastic skin like a twig of pretzel scraping the lining of a throat. It thunders above our heads—a herd of something hunted, eyes stuck open with adrenaline.

I yank my head up in fear at the sound, but when I look around at other faces for reassurance that I am not alone in my unease, they are still facing forward, listening to Elder Dave talk about how Christ is in our hearts. "Our *hawts*," he says in his middle-New Hampshire accent, dropping the growling edge of the *r* for something softer and more bucolic. Despite the electric hum of the Airmax, the congregation stays attentive, everybody twisting their necks just so, finding the angle that will help them drown out the sound of something filled with hot air.

A man is filled with something. He is on the floor near the back aisle, huddled into a fetal shell. The sun from a high window is causing a thin film of sweat to reflect off the carved dip of his temple. He looks up occasionally, his eyes empty—or, perhaps, overflowing—and his mouth is open like a snapped drawbridge. This posture is something parishioners describe as God working inside the person. He is, in the words of the more spiritually experienced in our church, "filled with the Holy Spirit"—that is, the swirling abyss between soul and body has been temporarily bridged, and this person is experiencing a direct movement of God in a physical way. Aside from causing the person to turn himself or herself into as much of a circle as possible, other Spirit-filled manifestations acted out by our church members include speaking in tongues, prophesying, and passing out—a phenomenon known as being "slain in the Spirit." The phrase is frightening at first, but then I can't help but want something from within, something so pure, so honestly palpable to literally knock me out with belief.

I am sixteen, and have not, at this point in high school, ever felt such a clear bodily connection with the Holy Spirit, though I am told that within me, the potential for bridging the gap is always there. Because of this, I can't help but assume that, even though I consider myself a Christian, something deep inside me must still be untouched, unsaved. I wonder what it would be like to rouse my soul and find myself (or lose myself) in this man's position right now, in plain view of everyone in the building—the dry smell of dirt hovering above the plastic tiles, a numbness entering just below the kneecaps and on my supinated ankles as they make war against the ground.

And the eyes.

I imagine the sting of the congregation looking back at me as a crouched potato, some content to see someone experiencing God and some wondering if the display is genuine, while others are jealous that it isn't happening to them, and others still that are scared that this *could* happen to them. This is my own progression of thoughts, however—no one else here looks scared or empty. It is the looks of others I am scared of. Because I can't know what lies in the heart behind those eyes, I interpret everything visually—if they look holy, then they must be.

Whenever we sing a song in church, my mother sees my inactivity and tells me it's ok to raise my hands or sing along. "You can close your eyes you know," she says, in the way she has told me many times before, as if the thought hadn't occurred to me. "No one is going to look at you." I have tried this, but there is an awareness that forms out of the darkness that everyone's head is turning to me, retinas aimed, shooting thoughts into their brains like, "Oh, good. He is finally getting it. He is finally filled."

The idea of eyes on my back—gazes slicing through the taut skin sloping over my shoulder blades and into my chest—turns up the heat, even as I stand there ostensibly unobserved.

The heat always begins in my temples—rhythmic thumps in my veins, which feel blood-bloated to the point of bursting. Then the sweat comes in flashing waves, as if the drops are being scooped out of my forehead and splashed onto my cheekbones. The flashes continue down to my armpits, drenched pulses pounding out a trance beat over my skin. A bead of sweat drains off the tip of my nose and falls to my feet. I am being emptied. "Or do you not know that your body is a temple . . ." writes Paul in 1 Corinthians 6:19 (ESV). But, how do I know what is being expelled, and what will fill the vacancy?

It is the fall of 1998, I am a junior, and I am in the backseat of Cathy St. Laurent's Lincoln, sitting cramped next to my girlfriend Cassy and her cousin, Jesse, a drummer who plays in the worship band with me. Cathy is driving with her daughter next to her, and Jesse's mom riding in the front passenger-side seat. We have just pulled into a Subway deli to order dinner. I am hungry, but not for a sub—especially not from a place I've been working at for the last year. We are on our way to Acquire the Fire—a Christian youth rally that tours the country annually, meeting in auditoriums packed to capacity with sweaty, nervous, excited teenagers looking to be filled with the Holy Spirit. I, however, can't shake off the awareness that for the first time, Cassy and I are next to each other in a dark car. Considering our respective sets of parents have strict rules about dating, this is the most alone we've ever been, and that fact alone has me sweating through two shirts, and possibly my coat. I have never kissed anyone, but never have the conditions been so promising. It occurs to me that if I were standing, I would most likely fall over.

"What kind of sub do you want?" she asks as she moves to get out of the car.

"Sick. Nothing for me," I say, and immediately feel the urge to keep talking, simply because of how close our lips are. "Gonna save my money for Denny's later anyway."

"Suit yourself," she says as she climbs out of the car, and I take my first full breath in over an hour.

When they return, I can smell the pickle juice about to drip off the side of Cassy's turkey and cheese on white.

"They loaded up on the pickles! Holy crap, I love pickles!" she says.

"You know, for a six inch, they're only supposed to put three pickles on."

"I asked for extra."

"Well, then they're only supposed to put six. Someone in there's gonna get a talking to when the food prices come in next month."

After ten minutes of silent chewing, the car relaxes into a hypnotic, highway-induced coma. Jesse has drifted off to sleep, and the only light is the trickle of electric green and red coming from the dashboard. I am sitting against the window, with Cassy on my left. She has started to lean against me, and I can feel her heat become mine and press into my temples in a familiar way. Soon, she is lying across my lap, looking up at me in a serious manner that says something I don't recognize. She pulls my face down close, and I am sweating. She kisses me, and I can feel the perspiration leaking through my T-shirt and onto my sweatshirt. I pull up slightly.

"I've never . . ." I whisper. "I mean, I don't know how to do this."

She doesn't answer and pulls me down again. The faint smell of pickles is on her lips, the taste of lip gloss and vinegar passing between us. It occurs to me that this should be gross, but instead is absolutely intoxicating, and my pulsing skull feels so full that it aches.

My high school organizes van runs each year when Acquire The Fire makes its New England stop at UMass Lowell. I did not attend when it came around during my freshman year, feeling incredibly anxious about large groups, especially groups committed to working themselves into a spiritual frenzy. When those who did go returned, their faces were all plastered with the same knowing grin. They were singing new songs in chapel, and they kept speaking of how hot the fire was within them. "I rededicated my life to God," they all said with the same phrasing, pitch, and tone. "I am on fire for Jesus. Are you?"

During my sophomore year, I went because my friends who had gone previously said there was a Denny's next to the hotel. I loved hotels, and I had only seen Denny's on TV. Though we would only be spending a fraction of our time using complimentary shampoos and eating omelets, somehow, these details sealed the deal for me.

I was still digesting my Grand Slam when we entered the auditorium for the first time. The blackness walloped me. There were lights, but they were low, wired with haunting bars of neon light. It felt as if we'd entered a KISS concert by mistake. I felt dehydrated almost instantly, as if the whole auditorium was there to drain me. Fog machines began to billow from the stage while the worship band plugged in their guitars and keyboards. From the first note on, the weekend blurred into a mass of waving human flesh— arms raised, eyes closed, bodies folded into eggs in the aisles. I cried at one point. I had no idea why, and this made me feel guilty. I never wanted to return.

But things changed when Cassy and I got together. Before my junior year, I had never had a girlfriend. Well, Keren asked me out, via a note, when we were freshmen, but she dumped me three days later, via another note, shortly after I told her that she gave me a reason to wake up in the morning. Cassy and I had passed the three-day mark, and I could hardly believe I hadn't scared her away yet.

"Are you going to ATF this year?" she asked.

"Well, it was kinda weird last year. But, what do you think?"

"We should go. Cathy said we could ride with her and Auntie Marie."

And once again, even though I knew the time in the car would be vastly overshadowed by the time in that quivering, spiritually orgiastic auditorium, I couldn't say no.

When we pull into the auditorium parking lot at UMass Lowell the next morning, I realize that the last thing I want to do is think about my relationship with God. I am burning, but I know it is not the kind of flame the group inside will want me to fan. Last night, we stayed at the house Cassy lived in before her family moved to New Hampshire this past summer. The house hadn't sold yet, so the empty space enabled us to save some money on hotel costs. Even though we were staying in separate rooms, I sneaked into Cassy's room to give her a good-night kiss, not considering that standing up and kissing posed certain hormonal consequences that had been easily concealable when seated in a car. Within the first second of contact, I started bending forward to at least diminish what was happening, terrified she'd think I was a pervert. As soon as I could, I ended the kiss with a 180-degree heel-spin and a muttered "good night." I crawled into my sleeping bag in the next room, curling into the fetal position to hide something I've only known to be ashamed of.

Even though she let Cassy and me sit next to each other in the car, somehow never noticing our covert vinaigrette-making, this morning Cassy's Aunt Marie says, "Now, Cassy, I don't want you and Bryan sitting next to each other once we get inside. I don't want you to miss what God has in store for you."

The seats in the auditorium are painful, and the darkness is swollen. The air is thick with the burnt, wet smell of fog machines, their chemical clouds spewing into the balconies. It is so humid that I hope the crowd will be able to distinguish spiritual ecstasy from heat exhaustion. I am not sure I will know the difference.

The service starts with a roar, and just like last year, the flesh begins waving as soon as the first guitar chord is strummed. That haze of shock is on me again, and I cannot tell what anyone is saying until Ron Luce, the keynote speaker, gets up. He makes a quick joke, citing some pop cultural reference that sends streams of smoky laughter across the arena. "Hey! This guy really *gets* us," they seem to be saying. I start to laugh, too, not wanting any heads to turn my way, but I stop when I breathe in and all I can smell is bad breath—a corporate case of halitosis that has originated far below.

Ron launches into his first speech the same way all of his subsequent speeches will go—starting quietly, building to a crescendo, then emphasizing his final point with a forced whisper, as if to suggest he's getting choked up. It doesn't have to make sense—the audience is so worked up with hopeful anticipation that he could yell, "Mashed potatoes!" and be met with raucous applause, kids fainting in their chairs.

Even though nothing of what he is saying sticks in my head, I feel overwhelmed with guilt. I would rather be kissing a girl with pickle breath then strengthening my faith. When I feel guilty, I feel empty, but I'm not sure it's cause and effect so much as that the two sensations are synonymous. Every time someone around me cheers or yells "Amen!" I am reminded that I don't feel what they feel, so I must be empty. And if I am empty, then that is nothing to be proud of. It is at this point that I start to hear Ron's words.

He moves into what rallies such as this refer to as the "altar call"—the period of the service where the audience is invited to publicly accept (or reaccept) Jesus into their hearts. Like any kind of sales pitch, his call plays on heightened emotions. Ron's brow moist with sweat, his entreaty goes something like: "If any of you tonight are feeling something stirring within you, something urging you to confess to God that you have gone astray, and that you are feeling empty, then I urge you to stand up in your seats and pray with me." The temple-throbbing in my head starts up again. I imagine what it would feel like if I stood up before the guy next to me does. He'll think I've really screwed up my faith if I'm so anxious. I look over at him, and as his head turns away from me, I catch a look of tired confusion in his fading eyes that I almost find kinship with. "Don't worry about people staring at you," Ron continues, somehow tapping into my inner dialogue. "Even if you've already given your life to Jesus before this night, I ask you to look into your heart. What is God telling you?" He goes on, suggesting that perhaps God may be telling us that we have not been faithful lately, and that perhaps we need to make a point of showing our peers that in order to be filled with the Holy Spirit, we should rededicate our life to God . . . right now.

I'm one of the last to stand. It may be that the schoolmates and others around me are just as nervous, or that those who stood up immediately are just being spiritually showy, but I can only see what is happening on the surface: they are standing, and I am not. I wonder if Cassy is standing, but can't spot her through the fog. Ron keeps saying, "No pressure, no pressure," but it is a form of reverse spiritual psychology. He is really saying, "There is only pressure, and I will crank it up until it breaks you." I know that next year, Ron will return with the same message, renewing our faith like a subscription to *Rolling Stone*. He says something to those still seated about not knowing when our time may be up in this life. You could walk out of here and be hit by a truck. Would you be ready to face God right now? That guy next to me is still seated and looking towards me again, but I only catch his glance in my periphery. I want to ask him if he feels this weird urge too—this guilt that is telling him to stand but only so he won't be ostracized later when everyone's talking about "what God did in there." Other eyes ping towards, around, through me, everyone looking for what they should do, and I interpret their looks perhaps the same way they are misinterpreting mine: "Hmph. Look at him there, full of sin." So, with sweat trailing down the sides of my rib cage, I stand up.

The thing is, the only quantifiable fact in the auditorium is that most people's knees are functional. There is no consequence for our physical declaration like there would be in places like Sudan where I've learned that persecuted Christians need only place a drop of spit on a picture of Christ to recant their faith and thus save them from being shot on the spot. Here, our standing will allow Ron to report massive success back to his organization, Teen Mania, and to display staggering percentages on his subsequent marketing materials that will no doubt gather groups this large and force the same reaction.

"Look around you!" Ron yells as he opens his eyes, reveling in the glory of a crowd that is now fully on its feet, for one reason or another.

It is customary for a speaker that visits my school or church to give their testimony on how they got saved, or, another way to say it: "How I got full." They usually start with a brief description of their life before Christ, typically involving some kind of earthly vice—drugs, wealth, sexual promiscuity—and how, despite the high they felt from such activities, they were left feeling empty.

But they're full of it.

In these contexts, feeling empty tends to be a phrase used towards the aim of telling everyone what reversed the emptiness. Rarely does anyone spend any length of time communicating what being empty is actually like, or if such a state is even possible.

What these hyperbolic converts don't get is that being filled with God's Spirit is actually a violent emptying of your own spirit. You were in spiritual need because you were too full of rot, not because there was some "God-shaped hole" in your chest.

I don't have a testimony, and I'm frightened that someone at school will ask me to share it sometime, forcing me to say something like, "In a first-grade Christian education class, I mouthed a prayer along with our teacher and became a Christian." But then, I'll stop and think about it longer before continuing with, "Wait; in fifth grade a different teacher led me in a similar prayer. And then I was baptized at age ten." I know this because it was my idea. My family and church stood and watched as I was immersed in the June cool waters of Lake Winnepesaukee. "But then, in eleventh grade I accepted Jesus as my Savior at a youth rally in a packed stadium at UMass Lowell." I will not tell them it is because I felt guilty for making out with a girl with pickle breath on the way to the arena, or that, given enough awkward silence, every head at the revival meeting will eventually turn to each side and assess the ratio of lifted to unlifted hands when the speaker asks if anyone feels empty. Inevitably, of course, groupthink will lead everyone's hand, including mine, to reach to the heavens, even if we have no idea why.

2

"Are you going to the prayer walk?" my friend Pete asks me as we walk back from the Gordon College cafeteria in the fall of 2001, his eyes downcast to achieve that tone of *if you don't say yes, then there is something wrong with your soul* that I have seen on countless teachers, parents, and pastors throughout my childhood. It is a tone that says, *You are not concerned about your role in the kingdom of God. You are not filled with the Holy Spirit.*

"What do you do during a prayer walk?" I know it is a stupid question, but I'm trying to evade answering his question directly until I get a few more details.

"Our chapter of Amnesty International puts it on every year. They give you a candle and you walk around campus praying for those whose human rights are being violated all over the world."

"Sounds dangerous," I say, deflecting again.

"Obviously you keep your eyes open," he says, annoyed. "So, are you going?"

That night, Pete and I are given candles, and a girl with a grill lighter gives everyone a light. I see cars passing our campus, our flames undoubtedly visible to them. I can't help but wonder what I would say if they asked what Gordon was up to this time.

"We're helping the poor and the less fortunate," I'd tell them.

"Do the poor need more candles?"

"No, it's to help me as I walk around campus in a continuous state of prayer."

"What do you say when you pray-walk?"

"I'm not sure. 'Lord, help the poor'?"

"Will that help?"

I have no idea, but I start walking anyway, trying to tune out the counterarguments. About ten minutes into the walk, I realize that rather than praying, I'm really focused on keeping my candle lit. And not only that, I've created some silent competition in my head that is keeping track of whose candles have gone out, feeling a strange sense of relief in the fact that these people who clearly know more about pray-walking than I do are still susceptible to being snuffed before reaching any grand conclusions. Metaphors of fire are so common within Christian youth culture that it's now impossible for me to not see the flame as a literal manifestation of spiritual fervor. The longer I burn, the more holy I hope to become. As I approach the end of the prayer walk there is not a single thought in my head except making it to the end intact, and the only prayers I've managed to complete are in regards to keeping the candle aflame.

Despite my best attempts to not take it seriously, and my unsettling lack of compassion for a global plight that I can only understand in the abstract, there is something about my willful silence that levitates my mind. I wander back to my room, alone, convinced that I have taken part in something soul benefiting, and decide that, in the morning, I'll continue the solitary walk, hoping that God isn't quite through with me yet.

Nobody is ever empty. "I will remove from them their heart of stone and give them a heart of flesh," God tells the Old Testament prophet Ezekiel concerning the exiled nation of Israel. When someone says they are empty, they are really a walking stone. Instead of reckoning with the cold, heavy heart in their chests, they imagine themselves as a hollow shell, their damp, lumpy inner life having been sucked out by a predator who leaves the shell to drift until it is crushed, or sometimes, saved.

I am not empty, but I am in exile.

There is a reason why revivals—from the Great Awakening to Acquire the Fire—always seem to be either coming or going, and never last long. People feel empty, so they want the opposite. Revivals allow for a fleeting feeling of fullness via the inspiring inflection and definitive fist pounds that punctuate buzzwords like, "Repent! And be saved!"

But it is impossible to sustain the sacred butterflies in your stomach. Their wings close and decay. They are eventually swept off by the blinking wings of the monstrous half-beings that Ezekiel sees in a holy vision. They are a type of angel called cherubim—a word that we've turned into some kind of doll-like figure in the Precious Moments style. But they are anything but celestially comforting. As Ezekiel fearfully describes them in chapter 10 of the book that bears his name:

Their entire bodies, including their backs, their hands and their wings, were completely full of eyes, as were their four wheels. I heard the wheels being called "the whirling wheels." Each of the cherubim had four faces: One face was that of a cherub, the second the face of a man, the third the face of a lion, and the fourth the face of an eagle.

At the postulated time this passage was written, the people of Israel were living in exile, and their temple in Jerusalem was empty—or at least, not filled with its rightful contents. In his vision, Ezekiel watched the cherubim, with their whirling, watching wheels, escort the Spirit of the Lord out of the Temple in gruesome, holy exodus.

Jesus does the same thing in the New Testament when he walks into church and sees commerce being conducted inside. He doesn't ask if they're feeling empty. He knocks over their tables and wares and says that they've turned God's house into a den of robbers. When he is verbally accosted afterwards by the religious leaders, he tells them, "Destroy this temple and I will rebuild it." He's talking about the structure in the foreground, but they miss that his use of *this* refers to the temple of his body.

Salvation is a process of constant destruction. It is not the hand that pulls you from the cliff, but the hand that lets you go so you can feel where your bones reset.

When the author and apologist C. S. Lewis finally gave in to Christianity after years of staunch atheism, he did not shout for joy or dance in the aisles of a sweaty stadium. He never liked the idea, but when he could refute it no longer, he resigned himself to it. As he forced himself into a kneel, no doubt one knee at a time, allowing for a few more seconds to come up with a reason why this was ludicrous, he described himself as, "the most dejected and reluctant convert in all of England." Only after destroying himself did he unexpectedly discover peace.

The leaves are dead, and they look like piles of thin-sliced roast beef. They crunch like toast as I walk along one of the many wooded paths that surround Gordon College. I am filled with the Holy Spirit. At least, this is what I keep saying to myself, and will continue to say it until something happens. It is a clear Saturday in April, and though it is not quite warm enough for the thin track jacket I am wearing, the heat from my forehead blankets my face from the chill. I am also light-headed, and I'm not sure if this means

I am in spiritual territory. Still, my eyes feel empty, and it's as if I'm staring into them from the outside, scanning for a better view of what's going on beyond my eyes. I must be filled with something, though it feels like nothing. I have not spoken to or seen anyone since last night's prayer walk.

As I walk through the woods, I step around whirling, track-laced puddles formed by four-wheelers, and I push my body into the tree cover like I am transporting a prisoner. I've had it with people telling me about their unique and powerful experiences with God, and when I ask them what it was like or how to do it, they just give me some secret society look and say, "You'll know when it happens." So, I've decided to make it happen by recreating common elements that seem to run through a lot of their stories. I am alone in the middle of God's creation, with all intentions of communing with it. I have been praying nonstop since the prayer walk, and have started repeating a buzz phrase from my church back home, "I am ready, Lord. Give me your wisdom. Let your Spirit work in me."

In the middle of a small clearing covered inches thick with crispy detritus, I pause and look up. I try and remember every clichéd spiritual phrase that I've ever heard coming from the lips of those lost in praise to God.

"You are the creator of blue, O Lord of hosts, and it is beautiful," I say out loud, staring at the sky. There is not a person within a half-mile of me at least, and yet I'm constantly scanning my periphery to make sure no one is hearing me. I have no idea what "Lord of hosts" means, but people have been saying it reverently my whole life. I look around again, and feel like someone has just caught me talking to a sandwich.

But I won't give up. I want to ingest creation; I want to be shoved by a miraculous punch of Holy Wind until I am running full speed and begin to understand what it means to feel eternity and not shudder in temple-thumping fear.

I look down at the beefy leaves. Without thinking, I bend over and grab two handfuls, the bottoms of which feel like soggy Raisin Bran. I shove the mass into my face, sniffing in its musky essence with gusto. I figure that if I can get close enough to nature, some kind of door will open, and I'll finally be allowed in. Or, perhaps I will be the one doing the opening.

I try anything that might help increase my chances. In the Modern Jewish Culture class that I am taking, I have learned that during times of *daven*, the general term for the Jewish practice of prayer, Orthodox Jews will rock back and forth, heel to toe, toe to heel, gaining momentum with every prayed phrase. The swaying is a result of a prayer life so intense that the body must respond physically to the movement of God within them. It works itself from the inside out, like a shard of glass burrowing its way out of skin, looking to once again be filled with the light of day.

So, with clumps of dead leaves still pushed flat against my face, I start moving, thinking maybe I can reverse the process and bend God's being into my body first and then my soul. Over and over I repeat, "Yes, Lord, yes," not quite sure of what I'm agreeing to, until a flake of stem snaps from its leafy corpse and is sucked into the back of my throat. "Oh *God*, I'm choking," I yell in a broken tone, flailing and hacking in an attempt to empty myself, not realizing until my airway is clear that I have fallen over, toppled like a corrugated pile of old, holy bricks.

But what about that wheel-within-a-wheel thing that Ezekiel saw next to the cherubim? Why does a winged creature need a set of wheels? They can go in all directions at once—the sound of eternity spinning its wheels. They helped carry the Spirit of God *away* from the temple, lugging it to those in exile. The Spirit has no home, and is on the move in search of its people, even if they had gone from *dominant* to *remnant*, wandering, hoping for a place to land and stop spinning.

I don't want a homeland, and I don't want to stop. You can swallow your testimony back into your throat and see if that doesn't make you feel full.

I want to be destroyed, as often as possible. I want to spin in all directions, overwhelmed by how eternity is made up of inexorably cyclical moments that somehow still change direction. If I stop now, the wheels will run me over.

[*A **tomb** is like a simile; it is a hollowed receptacle of approximate meaning. Even without ever having been behind the two-ton stone, you can start making guesses, theorizing about what it must be like inside that eternal dusk, hoping all the while that eventually the angel will come and roll it away, and you'll say man, I was way off. When Christ was raised from the dead, it was his absence that was discovered first: he wasn't in the tomb. He was dead and gone, and now somehow even more gone. Later, when he appeared to two of his followers, they didn't recognize him for hours, and right after the moment they realized whom they'd been chatting with, he disappeared again. When you are finally in front of the answer you're looking for, it disappears, and you're left tapping the side of your head, trying to come up with what the implications of the answer were really like.*]

13

What It's Like

It is in the tepid silence that I sin.

Sitting on my unmade bed in Beverly, Massachusetts, I am reading the Bible. It is the fall of 2005, and I have closed the door so that Aaron and Mariah, the married couple that Natalie and I have lived with for the last few months, won't catch me and think of me as some Bible-thumper holding onto the faith of my worm-tracked youth. I'm consumed by a verse in the Gospel of Luke where Jesus calls his first disciples. They are fisherman, and I picture the scene twenty miles north on the wharf in Gloucester, the smell of salty rot climbing the harbor as men in gut-streaked yellow coveralls drag the daily catch off their boats. The fishermen in Luke have been fishing all night in desperate hopes of making a drachma or two, but their nets come up empty, only the remnants of shell and barnacle clinging to their patched and repatched netting. Jesus tells them to let their nets down again, and they say, *that's crazy, but if you say so, guy,* and then their boats almost sink under the weight of the fish they pull up.

It's as if Christ has saved the day—clearly the fish will be enough to provide for the whole fleet for some significant length of time. At least, this is how it appears. The next thing he tells them is to leave it all there and follow him. And according to Luke, there's no hesitation, no period of silence where they picture how that fish money could finally patch the roof, could allow them to surprise their girlfriends with some of that expensive purple cloth that everyone's going on about. Instead, they just tie the boats to their moorings and latch on to the faith that's just baited their guts.

But on the bed, I am quiet, and I can hear the ticking of the gas stove and the cracking of eggs out in the kitchen. Whenever I read the Bible I put myself in the story, add my brown-headed, spectacled frame into the robe-and-sandal crowds. As Simon Peter and the other ex-fishermen start to follow, I stand and watch the wind pick up under their cloaks, my mouth opens like something inside wants to get out, to follow—but look at all that fish! They're just going to leave it there for anyone? I know enough to not go and claim what Jesus so clearly demonstrated was a fleeting, earthly treasure, but the dissonance between the two lives—sacred and secular, holy drifter and rich man—renders me unable to speak or turn my foot.

Making no noise and no movement, I'm like nothing.

I seem to like being a Christian. But, I'm wondering what the difference is between *liking being* something and *being like* something.

That narcissistically long word *verisimilitude*, with all its *I*'s looking back at itself, simply means "the likeness of truth," or the mere appearance of being true or real. It is the armature of reality, a façade, saying nothing of what populates the inner sanctum. The outer is not necessarily the inner, and though an appearance may be like something real, it cannot tell us the true state of things.

In my senior year of high school, my mother gives me a black-and-white WWJD ("What Would Jesus Do?") bracelet, and by now the fad has started to become an uncool accessory, even for Christian teens. But I wear it anyway, clasping the flat, cotton band around my wrist and tugging on the end until I feel my pulse push against the fabric. I have a bit of a problem with bracelets. It seems that if someone else wants me to wear one, then I have a hard time deciding when the time to release it has come. After hospital visits I typically let the plastic ID bracelet hang there for a month until it more or less gives up holding itself in a circle. I want people to see my determination, and on some level must want them to pity me for carrying around proof that I was sick, injured, and unable to accept the fact that I'm supposedly healed.

This bracelet is meant to be a reminder, that in every situation you can look at your wrist and think, "What would Jesus do?" It's a simple enough mantra that helps with those big, easy things—picking a charity to donate to, steering a conversation away from gossip, visiting a sick relative amidst a busy workweek. But let it trickle into everything, and picture Jesus: when he accepts change from the barista at Starbucks and eyes the tip jar, even though someone's told him that if the manager's around, they're legally not allowed to put that cup out; when he is so full after eating baked ziti, and there's not enough left for lunch tomorrow, and he can't eat another bite, so he should just throw it out, but what would his mother say?; when he considers inviting his brother over, because he lives alone, but he knows if he comes over, he won't stop talking, and he'll keep saying, "Mom always liked you best," and he'll have to say again, "No, no, that's crazy."

Over the five years I wear it—through college and then some—the bracelet shrinks and tightens from repeated showering, no doubt also turning into a personal petri culture. The black fades to charcoal, and if I twist it over, the underside shows brownish stains growing out from the buckle. It smells, it is going bad, and I'm just wordlessly letting it run its own life cycle. But I can't take it off, fearing the implications of discarding a reminder to let Christ's teaching dictate my every move. Plus, by this point, the bracelet has become so much a part of me that I barely notice it. So from the outside, it's still the likeness of truth: because I have faithfully worn this bracelet, it appears I have faithfully done what Jesus would do. Under that verisimilitude, though, lies a band of white skin that is softening with each shower, a slow spoiling of what I think faith is like.

Extended Simile 1: Like a Banana

It first happens in Laconia, New Hampshire, when I am somewhere between five and six, and hate bananas. This was not always the case. I liked them when I was four. But, a year or so later, I peel a streaky flap back to reveal a brown-veined fruit, curved and pale like the emaciated forearm of my emphysema-weakened grandfather.

It is over then and there—like nothing I've ever disliked before. It is an introduction to belief and doubt. Or, at least what they are like.

Things only worsen when I walk into the kitchen late on a Saturday morning and see a faded, lemon-colored Pyrex bowl with a potato masher sticking straight up from inside its exposed bowels. When I look over the edge, I see a viscous brown swamp, flecked with black. To the left of the bowl, there are the discarded skins of the fleshy, rotten bananas that Mom had left on the counter to go bad. I tried to throw them away the day before.

"Oh, no," she said. "I want them to go bad."

"You *what*?" I asked, holding the calloused tip of the bunch with as little of the pads of my index and thumb as possible, walking almost on my toes as if I am carrying an unstable bomb out of a crowded department store.

"I'm going to make banana bread with them."

"But they're rotten."

"I know. They're supposed to be."

I placed them back down and back away slowly, as if the bomb squad's leader has just said, "No, don't worry. We want that to explode in the middle of Sears."

The masher is stuck like the sword in the stone. I am amazed at the sludgy goo's resistance as I tug upward on the masher's ribbed hilt. When the lumpy mass relinquishes, it gives a *thwoosh*—a sound, I imagine, one would hear as a harpoon is pulled from the stomach of a stuck whale.

I stare at the innards encasing the base of the liberated masher, repulsed that though the brainy matter is caked and hanging off, none of it drips off the utensil's end. While I understand that making fresh what is rotten is resourceful, there is something about letting—no, *wanting*—the thing to turn bad before it is redeemed that strikes me as insane.

✕

The WWJD bracelet is still hanging on the year after I graduate college. By this point, Natalie and I have been married for over a year, and to save money, we've agreed to rent a house with our friends Aaron and Mariah. They once called themselves Christians, and some elementary voice inside me tells me that I can "help them" and bring them back to faith. There is rarely a night in the fall where I'm not out in the screen porch drinking Pabst Blue Ribbon with Aaron and Mariah. While he smokes American Spirits, Aaron talks and talks, effortlessly spouting off confident, seemingly airtight idioms that damn the rigid hypocrisy of the faith we grew up under.

"Look, the Bible is either 100 percent the infallible word of God, or else it's not, and if it's not, then it's a waste of time." He is sitting on a red rocking chair, his short, Nordic frame moving back and forth, his cigarette entering and leaving his mouth like a wooden bird in a cuckoo clock.

"No, that can't be right," I find myself saying, but struggle for the next sentence, the thoughts disintegrating into compost. There is a likeness of truth in what he's saying, disturbing as his proposition is. Aaron never lets colors bleed, and therefore he doesn't let colors fade. He was more of a rebel in high school, with psychedelic scenes of mushrooms painted on the walls of his basement bedroom that suggested more than just his music could be described as trippy. One night, however, he felt God stop his car on his way home and speak to him directly. So, like a good disciple, he left his Phish and pursued God wholeheartedly. He went on missions trips, he spoke in tongues, he led Communion. But he got disenchanted. "People don't really want to be changed by this stuff," Aaron told me. "If they did, they wouldn't act one way during the week, and then act like they're holy on Sunday."

He was completely right about that, but I think he's wrong about the Bible. I want to tell him that it'd only be wasted on us if it *was* perfect and infallible, because what good is something you can never live up to? This is where we differ though—even if I sense something is right, I don't sound confident, and I end up saying, "No, you're right, you're right," or, more likely, saying nothing at all, afraid that someone/Someone might still be watching me even through the smoky mesh of the back porch.

Extended Simile 2: Like Being Watched

On the way to school during my seventh-grade year, I notice a large, yellow van has been following our bus for the last twenty minutes. I lean over to Paul, who is sitting next to me and massaging a bag of Shark Bites fruit snacks, seeing if he can feel any of the larger "great whites" that have recently been added to the fleet.

"Yesterday I got three great whites," he says.

"The banana police are following us," I say, my head turning and my hand tapping his shoulder.

"That? No, that's a J. J. Nissen truck. I see them all around town."

He's right. I've seen them too. Just delivering hot dog buns to Quality Foods supermarket, I'm sure.

The bus takes a sharp right; I briefly see the broad side of my pursuer. The faint, red outline of the J. J. Nissen logo is there, but only because whoever removed it didn't do a good enough job.

"Oh, man," I whisper sharply to Paul. "It's not a Nissen."

"Well, it's still not that weird."

And it's not—at first. But I start to see the van once a week from then on, even up through college when I come home for breaks. Whenever I point it out, it always veers off just early enough for people to think I'm crazy for taking note of something so apparently insignificant.

It is like believing in God.

The realization that someone is actually watching is something I don't anticipate, despite sermons and dozens of Christian Education classes that spoke of faith in the unseen. I suppose I should have picked up the cues all along. In the car, my mother incessantly plays the cassette of Amy Grant's pre-mainstream, Christian music album, *Straight Ahead*, in particular, the song "Angels," where the chorus enthusiastically posits that angels watch over us. If this song had been about humans, say an ex-boyfriend named Chet (Chet is watching over me), then the sense of divine calling would've been replaced with a restraining order. It depends on the context.

In the same way, I suppose banana bread is like the resurrected Christ.

The idea that I believe in something omnipresent but unseen sounds more Hitchcock than holy. But this is just one example of what faith sounds like. I could just as easily say that it sounds like a body of water. I can't help but feel that similes are a desperate groping for the unattainable, a fevered attempt to define something through what, in our experience, it is like. If I were to make another frantic grasp at saying what God is like, I would—the word *would* being one more way to explain what I am like—say that it is like casting a net at random, hoping to ensnare a whole mess of fish, but coming up only with flecks of sea grass and crab parts. Then, based on the shards of shell, deducing what the fish—if I could catch them—would have been like.

Because the closest I can come to understanding the nature of God is through seeming similarities, I become obsessed with symbols. I am always looking over my shoulder and all around me to see if I can spot some kind of netted pattern. My mom decides to paint the house a light yellow. A yellow Jeep is for sale down the block from the house Natalie and I rent in Beverly after graduation. A year later, when we move to Rockport, one follows me to and from work every day. After Rockport, we move to New Hampshire, and there is one that belongs to someone in our apartment building.

"I'm beginning to think you'd like it if someone was actually stalking you," says Natalie as I point at the Jeep from the kitchen window.

"That's not like me, is it?"

"I think it's like you to like feeling picked out of a crowd."

"Well, yes, I guess I am like that."

"What if I had a tail?" my friend Ryan asks one night while we are drinking on the screen porch in Beverly. I laugh, but do not say anything. He is referencing a question he asked me when we were roommates freshman year.

Neither of us remembers anything else about that conversation, except that it was probably a funny one worth remembering and bringing up whenever we get together.

The tail question becomes a reminder, or maybe even a stand-in, for what living together was like. During a lull, I say, "You know, it seems like we never just answer questions, but instead just say what we'd be *like*, if we were actually answering them."

"Give me an example."

"Ok, like the 'What if I had a tail?' question. Do you remember what I said after you asked it the very first time?

"Well, you were like—"

"—That's just it! I was *like* something. Chances are I said, 'I'd be like, is that thing prehensile or are you just glad to see me?'"

"You definitely didn't say that. I'd have remembered that."

"No—you're right. It's too thought out. Wouldn't be like a real conversation of ours."

"So, is this a real conversation of ours, or just like one?" he inquires, his blue eyes darting up towards puttied strands of blond hair perched just beyond his own sight.

"Right now it's real, I think, but later when we talk about it again, we'll only talk about it in terms of what it was like."

"What if we tried that right now, then?"

"Tried what?"

"Talking about what this conversation is like."

"No. We're too close to it. It'd be like—geez, once you're aware of saying 'like' it's so hard to not say it. But, I don't know. Trying to say what this is like right now would be like trying to predict the future."

"But, later, you'll remember this differently than I will. When you report it back to me, I might say, 'I never said it like that.'"

"Exactly."

"Exactly what?"

"I'm not really sure anymore. I'm getting confused."

"Don't be like that." His smile curves, and I can't tell if it's out of annoyance, or out of the discomfort of being in a conversation that is always careening away from absolutes.

What frightens me is that an accurate assessment might be to say that what we are like is actually what we are, as if we've become apparitions of a few characteristics we demonstrated in the past, and have ceased to understand what it means to move our identities forward.

Extended Simile 3: Like Chicken

According to the Apostle Paul's Second Letter to the Corinthians, Christ "is the exact likeness of God."

Sitting down at Siam Delight with a few friends, I order a dish called Vegetable Noodle on the Beach and notice that you can add "fake chicken" for an extra dollar. I spring for it, to see what it's like.

"This tastes exactly like chicken," I say as a gelatinous thread hangs from my bottom lip. Natalie looks up and points at the extraneous matter so that I can remove it before anyone else notices. The rest of the crew pauses briefly, but no one responds verbally, as they're all pretty familiar with the near-constant commentary I make during gustatory excursions. After a few slurps of Tom Yam soup, they continue the conversation I interrupted.

But I'm consumed with likeness.

The suffix -ness takes a more concrete turn towards discovering the essence of a thing. But in the case of "likeness" it doesn't go the full transformative way—it only suggests that something is like something else. So does "likeness" mean "like the state of being like" or have I just thought myself into misleading circles?

I push through this question like reeds in a swamp.

No, like noodles on the beach.

No, I no longer want to know what it is like—I simply want to know what it is.

"What Would Jesus Do?" could be rephrased to "What Is Jesus Like?" and not really lose the meaning. In fact, every church service I've ever been to has been an attempt to answer this question. There is the implied hope that if we can find the right simile, we'll finally get *it*.

Christ is like: this bread, this wine, this cracker, this grape juice, this painting where he looks Italian and graceful, this painting where he looks Middle Eastern and in pain, this tree that bears fruit, this tree that is in the shape of a cross affixed above the pulpit, this baby doll wrapped in the likeness of swaddling clothes—the word "swaddling" never used except when describing what Christ's first outfit looked like, so that when we consider this likeness, we can compare it to the nativity recreation we saw down the street, or to one from last year; we can figure out what this experience is like stacked up against all the similar ones in the past, and hope that, if we move back far enough in our minds, we will stop saying "Christ is like," and finally just say, "Christ is."

Ephesians 4:14: "We will not be influenced when people try to trick us with lies so clever they sound *like the truth*"(emphasis added).

How, then, am I to determine what is truth, and what is the lie so compelling that it is truth-like?

Extended Simile 4: Like Oatmeal

My thinking on Monday when I first notice that my oatmeal tastes like blueberries is that my palate is evolving into that of a connoisseur. A tongue that is capable of discerning *hints* and *top notes*. With each mushy bite, I break down and isolate the elements:

1/4 cup of Scottish oatmeal, cooked in,

3/4 cup of water,

a few flecks of sea salt,

a teaspoon of local, unfiltered honey, and

2 tablespoons of rice milk stirred in at the end.

Well, this is Scottish style, not the typical rolled kind, I think, turning over and grinding the meal between my teeth, pausing for a moment to let a few breaths bounce between it and my tongue. It seems odd that a finer milling of the oats would unearth some latent fruitiness.

The honey—I've never had the unfiltered kind before, so perhaps it is more complex than the translucent store brand that comes in a plastic bear. I've heard that honey tastes different depending on what region it is cultivated in. Each globule contains a cross-section of the flora typical to the area the bees pollinate—a digested ecosystem, chewed and regurgitated. I've been told that eating a tablespoon of local honey every day is the equivalent of taking allergy medication. Perhaps these New England bees had found their way into a blueberry patch.

But the blueberry notes are a bit sharp—like a chemical mix that makes something taste like blueberry. It reminds me more of Fruity Pebbles than fruit; Boo-Berry, not blueberry. "It reminds me," I say. But a reminder is only a trapdoor into the memory of what a real experience was like. When I recently read the word "Duesenberg" I suddenly recalled a block of dialogue from the play *Annie*. I was Drake the butler in a high school production, and had to ask Daddy Warbucks if he'd be taking the Bentley or the Duesenberg. I started to feel again what it was like to be onstage, to remember rehearsed words and deliver them appropriately, to have makeup applied to my face with small foam wedges, to have my hair spray-painted gray and gelled so stiff it could've sliced pound cake, to share the stage with the girl I was dating when I auditioned for the play, but who had since broken up with me. But I am not in the play. I am on a seersucker-lined couch wearing moccasins and an old man sweater. Natalie is in the kitchen bleaching Tupperware that, up until this evening, contained food that smelled so evil it could have caused anyone to repent.

On Friday, after four days of eating the blueberry-ish breakfast, I am out of oatmeal and settle for a bowl of ten-grain hot cereal. The blueberry-ness is more pronounced then the other days, and I notice deeper layers of flavor. What is it like? It's familiar—something I've smelled previously—I scan my memory like it is a search engine: something from the night before. I had cleaned out the fridge and opened a tub of Country Crock that I knew didn't contain butter-like spread. Leftovers, but what is left over? I peel the lid back and breathe in deep as I see the lentil soup I made from a recipe out of *From Julia Child's Kitchen*. The smell is putrid, and reminds me that I had put ham in the soup—ham from Christmas, almost a month ago.

But that's it—the taste of gone bad. My phantom blueberry has revealed itself as horribly spoiled rice milk, meaning that for five days I've been drinking rot and didn't know it. It was a compelling lie, and I quietly ate it up.

In Revelation, the final book of the New Testament, Jesus dictates a series of messages to the book's writer, John, who is in exile on the island of Patmos. Each major church from John's time gets a specific letter addressed to them from Jesus, letting them know if they're moving forward or backward regarding their understanding of faith. While it's clear that many churches are getting stuff wrong, the passage that lodges itself in my head is what he says to the church in Laodicea: "I know all the things you do, that you are neither hot nor cold. I wish that you were one or the other! But since you are like lukewarm water, neither hot nor cold, I will spit you out of my mouth!"

The bathroom in our Beverly house is always cold in the morning, save for a few weeks in the summer. But, in late fall, the process of disrobing on the icy tiles and stepping under the showerhead is more like being put up to a dare than a morning ritual. As I typically do during the workweek, I try to make the shower last as long as possible, knowing that the chill that will grab me as soon as I turn off the knob will only crank up the anxiety of a new office job I've been struggling to make fit with the vision I previously had of my post-grad life. So, this morning, I bow my head and close my eyes under water that is losing heat fast, since I am not the first of four to take a shower. I let it gather in the thickness of my hair until it flows out slowly over my forehead like a mass of collected sweat.

As I lift my hand to the knob, the water by now like old tea, I notice a sheer white tan line on my wrist. I look down, and like a rain-surfaced worm, my bracelet lies curled by my foot. While my eyes were closed, the plastic clasp must have simply crumbled away, letting the band fall to the porcelain floor. When I pick it up, I see that the letters are so faded and mildewy that the hook of the *J* has been smudged into an *I*, and I wonder what I will do.

[*A temple* in the end is also a tomb, a vacant structure. It becomes holy only when you fill it with ideas and dreams. Like a late night car ride when you are young, being in a church has always made you sleepy, the rubbery edges of reality haunted by the blurry shapes of dream images that your brain wants to show you if you'd just give in and close your eyes. In church, your mother always points and laughs when she sees a bowed head still hanging low after the amen, and she nudges when it happens to you.

A visiting speaker, when making fun of church-sleepers like you, once followed up his joke with a sincere, "But, really, what better place is there to sleep than in the house of God?"

However, he never told you where you'd wake up.]

14

Wake, Sleeper

1

I am, with some hesitation, waking up. Though my eyes are still closed, a warm coil of sun is on them, turning the black behind shut lids to a liquid red. It will not be long before I give up and draw the lids back in the way the dust-stained shades of our house will soon be opened.

I have to pee so badly that my bladder feels like a filled-to-the-brim, thirty-two-ounce soda that someone has forgotten to put a lid on—I figure if I move at all, something will spill. I ignore the pain, knowing that if my eyelids unglue, I will not be able to fall back asleep. I also know that if my parents hear any movement upstairs, they will call up and make sure we are getting ready for church. At thirteen years old, I am well aware of all the factors at play on Sunday morning—every last detail that can be read as either implying that we'll be going to church, or that, by some miracle, we won't be.

Church starts at 10 a.m. It takes fifteen minutes to drive there, meaning we should leave at 9:45. But, ideally, my parents will want to arrive a little early so Dad can help Karl set up the folding chairs, and my mom can talk about Tupperware parties or ladies weekend retreats with Candace, Carol, Karen, and other church lady names. To make sure we have enough time, they will wake us up at 8:45.

Because the heat feels so intense, I wonder what time it is. *Maybe it's past nine*—which would mean that, for some reason, we won't be going to church today. This thought slides my face across the pillow, scratching and flaking off the dried drool, until my head is bobbing slightly over the edge of my bed. I am listening for movement, for slipper steps on the kitchen's cream linoleum, for the sheeting flow of shower water in the buried, awakened pipes. If I draw in and hold my breath, I can focus enough to discern the drip stream of hazelnut Folgers striking the bottom of the glass carafe like slow brush strokes on a snare drum.

All is quiet.

I reel my head back onto the pillow, pushing my face into its bosom. I begin opening my eyes, feeling the silken resistance of lash against sheet. It is easier to remain in the passive darkness rather than willingly be consumed by the shocking light. My head turns up away from its soft shroud and the objects of my room float in a suspended glow. One by one, they become rooted again; posters of the Beatles and Oasis tack themselves back onto the wall.

The room is so sun swollen that I think I've left my ceiling light on. Why do I try to explain away this irrefutable light with something man-made?

I reach under my bed, searching for my clock. It is only 8:35. Almost as if they were waiting for me to realize this, the pipes veining the walls hiss with water, and I hear the creaking steps of my dad approaching the front door. He heaves the wooden door from its resting place, and the storm door yelps as he pushes it open. With a percussive series of leafy shuffles, he picks up the inches-thick Sunday edition of the *Laconia Citizen*.

I lie to myself and think that there is still hope. My parents always get up early, and we're allowed to sleep in slightly longer since Allyson left for college a year ago. I tell myself there is a chance that at quarter of nine, my mother won't start climbing the stairs after her shower to wake up Caleb and me. I become aware of the soft ticks of my clock, so quiet and deferential when I went to bed, but now throbbing through the seconds. Something winces deep inside with the guilty realization that I don't want to go to church—that I never do. I start talking to God:

"But, it's not that this has anything to do with you," I think. "It doesn't say anything about belief or doubt, you know." I pause in between each sentence, like I would for any conversation. "It's not like I'll go to hell because I don't look forward to attending a church that has only one other preteen in it. It doesn't help that that one other person wears a T-shirt that reads 'Satan Sucks' every Sunday." I give room for responses, and though I am answered only with silence, it doesn't make me think that no one is listening.

I try to picture God. The pictorial flashes are culled from sermons, classes at school, illustrated Bibles for children, and as they start to fill my mind, contradictory versions rub against each other—Christ as the good shepherd but also a sacrificial Lamb, as the Son of God and also the Son of Man. In the moment these descriptors are offered to me, the point is clear, but later all versions take up the same amount of headspace, and none rise to the top as definitive. At thirteen, the vision I prefer is the one I have made up where God is an old farmer in faded flannel, hearing what I'm saying as he rocks on a celestial porch, grinning ever so slightly as if to say, "I know, I know." It is just as easy to see him in one of the other versions that have taken root—as a Zeus-like shadow of robes, judgment like wine pouring out of a goblet, nothing I say ever holy enough.

Even though these are scenes that I script and stage, the images feel potent, as if they have been injected via heavenly hypodermic. But there is a haunting voice that tells me I am making all this up. I haven't actually vocalized anything, but the dialogue is gaining layers of would-be voices saying, *you're wrong / I believe / you doubt*, until everyone is talking at once, anxious about the fact that there is no way to resolve this. "Look, eventually I'll find a church that I want to go to, ok? I promise."

Then I hear it—a muffled sock against carpeted stair, followed by the slight drag of a fleece bathrobe. I turn quickly to the wall, pull the blankets up to my nose and pin my eyes closed.

"Wake up sleepyheads!" my mom says on her way up. She is clapping as she goes in to rouse Caleb, and she starts singing, "Good morning / good morning / good morning / it's time to rise and shine!"

She claps and sings her way into my room in hopes of making me move. She will not leave until I can at least drone the words, "I'm awake,"—a grunt will not cut it. She throws back my covers and wrings her wet hair onto the small of my back, and I convulse—this is not how I want to see the light.

"I'm awake! I'm awake! Good *lord*."

"The Lord *is* good!" she says. Now that the confession has been forced out of me, I know that there is no turning back. "Ok!" she says, heading back down the stairs, "Don't you fall back asleep."

That night, as I wait for sleep, I stare at a poster of a Wings-era Paul McCartney on the ceiling above my bed. Though it is dark, the moon casts a dull sheen over the top of my pulled shade. It shines a dim spotlight on

Paul's greying mullet, looking like a tabby cat is resting on his shoulders. He has a Rickenbacker bass slung across his torso, but he is not playing it in this picture. Instead, he has his right hand raised, with eyes toward the not-pictured audience, his mouth opened like he is saying, "Good night, Berlin!" rather than singing the line, "Maybe I'm a man who's in the middle of something that he doesn't really understand."

Sleep is not coming easily tonight. I am dwelling on a conversation I overheard at church, where someone said, "Sometimes, doesn't it feel like your prayers are just hitting the ceiling and bouncing back down?"

I had not thought of this.

There are all those nights over the years where I kept myself awake asking forgiveness for every sin I could remember committing, forcefully pressing my eyes shut until the pinched corners of the lids rippled, desperately fighting the urge to sleep in the middle of a prayer, but failing. Now, I am afraid that if I don't say "amen" I'll wake up the next morning and technically still be praying when I tell my mom that I want Honey Nut Cheerios for breakfast. And then, as the day progresses in a suspended prayer, I'll most likely sin, seeing as how my friend Levi has procured a copy of the teacher's edition of our eighth-grade math book. Is it possible to sin while still asking forgiveness?

To avoid these supernatural contingencies in my nightly prayer, I always include, "And please forgive anything that I forgot, or haven't yet realized was a sin."

But this idea of not making it through the ceiling—requests and regrets uttered, then pushed back down the dark hole of my throat as if they had never been spoken. How many times has my heart not been in the right place? What is the right place? How many prayers have stopped at that picture of Paul McCartney?

This revelation has left me feeling particularly penitent as I think back over my more recent possible transgressions. After playing rag ball soccer in gym class at Laconia Christian School on Friday, I pulled out a new sweatshirt that carried the logo of Duke University. I hadn't made it outside the gym foyer before Mrs. Larousse spotted me through the black aviator sunglasses she wears all the time, regardless of cloud or roof cover.

"Hey!" she yelled, and started marching in my direction, dressed in her typical black pants, black turtleneck, and black windbreaker. If I had just met her, I would've thought the school had hired Roy Orbison to be our athletic director. "What is that you're wearing?"

I paused and looked down, still half hoping she was going to compliment my new shirt. I studied the picture on it—a blue devil, Duke's mascot—and realized I had made a huge misstep.

"Um, it's Duke. They're my favorite team—in college anyway." She clearly wanted to chime in at this point, but I kept going in order to deflect what I knew was coming. "My favorite NBA team is the San Antonio Spurs. You know? With David Robinson? Did you know he's a Christian?"

"Does your mother know you're wearing that on school grounds?"

"Well, she bought it for me."

"But there's a big devil on it! What kind of testimony are you giving to everyone who looks at that? Do you think that shirt is pleasing to God?"

Pleasing to God. Before her question, as long as I wasn't stealing from the candy pick-a-mix in the supermarket, or giving my brother forty lashes with the belt of a bathrobe, I figured that I was pleasing to God. I had assumed that a shirt had as much spiritual import as a pancake, so the idea that apparel choices could reflect badly on my eternal soul ratchetted up the anxiety swelling behind my sternum.

"I guess I hadn't thought about that."

"Well, take it off right now." She pulled a pen out of her jacket pocket and produced a rectangular pad of paper. "I'm giving you a pink slip so that your parents know about this."

"But they do know about this."

"Here," she said, tearing the slip off its gummy spine and handing it to me. "Bring this up to the office. It's just a warning this time. I won't give you a detention."

"Thanks."

"No problem, bud." Despite her futuristic nun style of dress and discipline, Mrs. Larousse has always had a soft spot for those who disobey. Her anger never lasts that long, and she's always quick to start joking around again. This turn of events made me feel like I do when I attempt to pray—guilty, but inexplicably accepted.

As I stare at a moonlit McCartney, I hope that Saint Paul won't hog all the requests this time, but will instead pass them on to someone who might actually listen.

2

In college, I attend a late-night service called Catacombs, held on campus every Sunday at 10 p.m. It is not a church service, they make clear, but rather a quiet time of hymn singing and introspection. There are no lights on in the campus chapel, and there are only a handful of musicians playing unplugged—a baby grand piano and cello throbbing out nocturnal cave paeans that have lines like, "Prone to wander / Lord I feel it / Prone to leave the God I love."

I am here because I have stopped going to church and praying at night almost altogether, and I feel damned. The last few times I've tried the nightly intercessions, I never made it far before drifting into sleep. I would awaken in the middle of the night to go to the bathroom, my hands still folded though the knuckles slack, the knot of fingers like snapped strings on a violin. I have become too aware of the fact that when I'm praying, it is no longer just me talking to God—it is a discordant summit of voices that spiral deeper and deeper, each one questioning the statement before it. It is as if my prayers have become stones that I am dropping down a well, to see how far they will drop, to listen for the splash that echoes back: will it be a plink or a flood?

Tonight, I am lying down, face into the scratchy upholstering of one of the far back pews in the chapel. When I close and open my eyes, there is no change in the blackness—I could be in a church or a tomb, falling or standing, comforted or buried in the darkest night of the soul imaginable. The decay of an E minor fades until there is just the slightest suggestion of dissonance, of vibrations fallen out of sync before they too disappear into the thick primordial tar. A voice speaks, "Thy word is a lamp unto my feet," and I think, *you can only ever see the next step, never what's actually in front of you.* Then my mouth opens, draws in black breath, and I fall asleep.

Five years after I graduate college, I take to drinking a spot of whiskey before bed, in order to slow my brain down and help me sleep. It occurs to me that drinking for some kind of practical outcome is not a good sign. When Natalie and I first moved to this apartment in Dover, New Hampshire, I tried over-the-counter sleep aids, but they didn't start working until the morning, and left me with a viscous blanket over my brain until dinner that day.

The whiskey doesn't really sit well with my acid reflux, so I realize it's only a temporary, somewhat romanticized fix. I know that, in the end, I'm just going to have to endure the chaotic liturgy of an uncorked brain.

It is Saturday night, and Natalie is getting ready for bed. I am still working—grading a student's essay for the college I now teach at while studying for my master's degree—and for a moment I contemplate staying up late. But if I want any kind of fighting chance at getting to sleep before midnight, I've got to go to bed at the same time as her. The reasons for this do not make me look so good. Put baldly: I like to cuddle, and I'm afraid of the dark.

So, I stop working, and as I brush my teeth, I let my eyelids sag, hoping they'll get the message and start closing. I go to the bathroom knowing that in thirty minutes, when I think I'm almost about to fall asleep, my brain will say, "Wait—do you have to pee?" And so, I'll let my body do whatever it is that it does to send a message from brain to bladder asking, "Anyone in here?"

Sure enough, shortly after climbing into bed, I start over-thinking the question of whether or not I need to pee again until I'm pretty sure that I do. Then, I second guess myself, and say, *aw—it's not that bad*, in hopes that this won't interrupt the delicate wait for sleep a little while later. But, then I'm consumed with thoughts of the inevitable—I *will* have to pee at some point. So, it might as well be now. By this point, I'm pissed. I throw the blankets up and storm into the bathroom, almost waking Natalie, but only enough that she turns on her side and continues to lightly snore.

This is the other problem.

She is by no means a chainsaw, though there are the occasional guttural spikes in volume. Rather, it is a slight wheeze through the nose—she claims she has to breathe through her nose to fall asleep. On days like this one, when allergies have congested her enough to give her minor trouble dozing, she'll place her hand over her mouth, putting her index finger between her septum and upper lip—like she is miming having a mustache—and apply the slightest, tugging pressure. I have no idea if this actually works, or if she just believes it does. Either way, she looks like she is in deep, but peaceful thought; it's annoying but also endearing.

From the second our heads hit the pillow, it is a race against the snore. I am wide awake, and know that she is utterly exhausted from another day at the human services agency where she offers staff support to clients with various mental or developmental issues. Though she doesn't normally work on the weekends, she had to help with a walkathon that the company and their clients were signed up for. On Friday, she spent most of her day running around the ER with a client that had an infection on her ass. And while today's event was easier than a normal day at work, the weight of her week doesn't make her sleepy so much as it knocks the wind out of her.

By contrast, my greatest challenge today was when the printer ran out of paper in the middle of a printing job, forcing me to take a minute to refill it. It isn't surprising that she's tired and I'm not.

Our heads laid to varying degrees of rest, I try to get her to talk more about her day, as this will allow me more time to get drowsy. She usually knows what I'm up to, and I sense this, so I try to make it a bigger deal.

"You know, this is our one time of quiet where we can just talk. Can't you just tell me a little about work?"

"This is not the only time. You could've asked when I got home."

"I was making dinner! Plus, you know me; I'm bad with formalities. I figure the topic will come up naturally."

"Well, it did. But it's too late."

"Don't make it sound like I don't care about your day."

"I didn't say that. It's fine, I'm just tired."

Though I've started to feel upset, I know that what I'm up to is a ruse at heart, so I drop the subject.

There is some drumbeat in my head, and I can't quite place it. There are not a lot of cymbals in it—just a fairly basic 4/4 beat, with some snare hits on the offbeat. I play it for four measures in my head, trying to discern its origin.

"What song is this?" I ask Natalie, after I can't figure it out. "*Bum-bum-tss-bum / tata-bumbum-tss-bum.*"

"You're kidding."

"It's driving me crazy!"

"I don't know! Just close your eyes and go to sleep."

"You know it doesn't work for me like that. If I close my eyes I have to concentrate on keeping them closed. Then, forty-five seconds later I notice that they've opened again."

"Well, then, you're not normal."

"Wait! It's one of *your* songs! The one about the down comforter."

"'Favorite One'?"

"Yeah—that's it. I've been trying to think of a good bass part that would go with that beat, and—"

"Look, I really am too tired for this. We'll have to talk about it tomorrow."

"But I'm excited about it now."

"Well . . . don't be."

She rolls over, and within a minute I hear her breathing change. I continue to listen as her breathing fades into the creaking of the pipes, the wind hitting a flagpole outside, the Cocheco River sloshing against rusty boats—noises that seem designed to enhance the silence of night.

There is a swelling burn in my chest as I realize that tomorrow is Sunday, shortening my breath as a hot thought forms the word *church*. It seems to have been there all along, waiting calmly for a moment of silence. I look over to Natalie in desperation, hoping that there is something I could bring up that wouldn't make her grumpy. There are no more distractions.

The feeling is one of paralyzing, chronic guilt. Of one that says, *You are all talk. If you actually went to church, you could probably stop complaining about not being able to find your faith.* I realize that every conversation I've ever had about faith has been one of expectation—that by telling people I am earnestly searching it means that I am. I've had seventeen years of biblical education, and I can quote maybe two verses in their entirety, despite the fact that I earned A's on every memorization test I took in high school. I can't even remember all the books of the Bible.

Come friends and children and let us tell

The halls of my head are being opened, and they smell musty, as if brown floodwater washed through its passageways years ago, leaving the stacked volumes of memory in a fuzz of green mildew, filled with graying blots of indecipherable ink.

The books of the Bible we know so well

When my parents retiled the kitchen floor, the carpenter let Caleb and me draw pictures on the plywood before he covered over it. I drew a clipper ship with seven sails, oars dipping into waves like rows of closed eyelids. I imagine that drawing now, sealed for fifteen years, blurred and smudged by the linoleum pressing down under our walking feet and the cold granite winter seeping up in through the floor.

Genesis, Exodus, Leviticus and Numbers, Deuteronomy and Joshua and Judges. Ruth and Samuel, Samuel and Kings, Kings and Chronicles and Chronicles. Ezra, Nehemiah, Esther, Job, PsalmsProverbsEcclesiastes

This is as much of the old children's song that I remember. Here's why this fact isn't all that surprising:

Ecclesiastes 1:11: *We don't remember what happened in the past, and in future generations, no one will remember what we are doing now.*

In a recent conversation I had with my father-in-law, he was excited that Natalie and I were going to visit a new church.

"It doesn't have to be perfect, you know," he told me. "You don't have to agree with everything they say, as long as they're at least trying to preach the Bible."

"But if I just sit there, and they say something I disagree with—and not just that, but am offended by—then how am I supposed to just ignore that?"

"You know what you believe. You don't have to let what others believe make you mad. They have a faith of their own, too."

"That's the other part of it. I sit there getting all up in arms about some disparaging remark against 'the homosexuals' but then I feel guilty for playing their own game of hating what they don't understand. I don't even know these people and I want to stand in front of them and—well, I'm not sure what I'd do."

"Sounds like that could be part of the problem you're having."

It turned out we could barely make it through the service at the church we visited. Set in an old car dealership, all the windows were blocked, curtaining out the bright winter sun that was trying to shed light on us. The sermon was about pornography and how it was wrong. Seemed a bit like low-hanging fruit for the churchgoing crowd.

"I want to say right now that we are an anti-porn church," the pastor announced through his headset microphone, his arm raised like he was under oath. *Are there any pro-porn churches?* I wondered. He proceeded to get the congregation all hot and bothered about how perverted our movies and television shows had become.

"Have you seen the *Family Guy*?" one woman yelled while the pastor drank water from a Dixie Cup.

"Should be banned!" came the answer from a raspy mother's voice across the room, feeding the kind of call-and-response group mentality I associate with lynch mobs.

Just when I thought they were about to start handing out torches, a delivery man walked in the main entrance, right as the pastor was saying, "Now, some couples use porn to help spice things up in the bedroom. And it works . . . for a while—" When he saw the intruder, he stopped abruptly and yelled out, "Sir, you look like you're in the wrong place."

It turned out that the man was making a delivery to the food pantry that the church kept for the poor in the area. If anyone in that room was physically doing something to help the "fallen" world we were living in, it was he. But the pastor had said what I was thinking: *I am in the wrong place.*

I haven't told my father-in-law about this experience. It is easy to tell someone why you didn't like a certain restaurant: "The service was bad," you could say, or "They wouldn't leave us alone. Kept asking if we were ok."

I want to tell him that, "The service was bad," but I'm going to have to find a way to back up this statement. And it can't simply be a matter of taste, either.

"You can't just customize a church that's everything you want," I can hear him say. "It's not all about you."

He's right. But in my head, it is all about me, because I'm the one with the problem. Everyone that I see at these churches seems to have figured out, or at least know how to act like they know, why they continue to go to church. Sunday morning comes, and they're up, turning on the coffee machine, making their children tuck in their shirts and taking care not to forget their Bibles as they rush out the door. Regardless of what spiritual battle may be clanging in their skulls, outwardly, they have made their choice.

So, the question that has been pupating inside me all day, every day, waiting for the night to fall so it can hatch and its spiky tendrils can crawl up my rib cage until I have no choice but to either consider it, or else be fully aware that I'm ignoring it, is:

God still exists. Why do you care?

I have to come up with something. I concentrate on the fan's whir, hearing a slight rattle as a screw comes a little loose from its housing. I wonder if the words I hear my father-in-law say actually reflect the mind of God. I start to half-pray, looking for some kind of validation that will say it's not wrong to not go to church. I mention that I've heard there are churches on the West Coast that were started by artists. *Why is there nothing like that in New England?* I hear the words of various visiting preachers from my childhood, calling New Englanders the "frozen chosen." But not to worry, many of them said, revival—"an astonishing move of God"—was about to descend on us. Sitting at church on those days, I looked up to the ceiling, then down to all the drooping heads and slack arms of the congregation. A few eyelids opened a bit wider, but only for a moment, as if they had been dreaming but were awakened suddenly by a car screeching in the distance.

"Any time now," the preacher promised.

"Any time now," I repeat, shuffling the blankets, and turning over onto my side.

Sunday morning wakes me with a start. It is after nine, and for a brief second I think that we won't go to church today. But I look over at Natalie, asleep, her hand still draped thoughtfully over her mouth, and then I remember that of course we won't be going to church. We haven't gone in months, and the few times we have gone, it has been on visits back home, or the occasional vain attempt to find one on our own. Since graduating high school, I've never belonged to a church. There was one place in Cambridge, Massachusetts, that I liked for a while, but mostly because of the free bagels.

I think about waking Natalie to say, "Hey—let's try that old Episcopalian church downtown," but I don't go through with it. A thought pricks my forehead, an aching memory of the panic that had kept me awake the night before. I hear footsteps in the apartment above us. They sound like shoes, nice ones with wooden soles that crack and fade as they move from one end to the other. I know that they are not churchgoers, and wonder why they have enough discipline to get up, and why the last thing I want to do is pull my face from the pillow. What is it like to wake up on Sunday and not think about church?

I put the thought out of my head and listen to the fan. The room is freezing, and I want to get up and turn the fan off. The sound has sliced itself deep into my ears though, and I can't help but dissect its tones. When I lie on my right side, it sounds like a hum coming from outside. Is it? I lift my head and hear tinny treble swirls layer themselves on to the low bass drone.

Beyond the fan a stronger wind gathers. It starts with a whistle at the far end of our apartment, in the kitchen, and then blows through the darkened, creaking boards that lie just below the floor and behind the painted sheetrock. *The wind has more than one tone*, I think as I try to follow its screeching course. *It is like guilt.* It coils itself around and through the dead wood, leaving phantom pains groaning everywhere it has touched.

Following the breeze, a car motors down my street and audibly slows down as it nears my building. It seems almost every car that passes does this. The street is one-way, with perpetually vacant parallel parking spaces lining the right side. Many of these cars will drift through each space as if they are trying on sweaters, searching for just the right fit.

I'm amazed how often, when I hear an approaching car, I turn to the window above my bed and watch their inertia set in. I imagine that my apartment is the site of some gruesome accident, each one of the passengers looking for a body, revolted when they find one, or disappointed when they don't.

I watch as one car pulls into every spot, brake lights flashing whenever it finds the centers between dozens of white lines. It is the appearance of stopping. There is not a single car parked on the whole road, leaving close to twenty successive spaces open for the car to choose, and every time this happens, I think it's an isolated incident. But over and over cars airily wend their way over the lines as if it's a ballet that everyone except me knows the routine to.

Stop already, I keep thinking as I stare at the passengers in the drifting car. Still, they roll on until they reach the intersection at the end of our street. Instead of braking, they accelerate with the confidence that only leaving something behind can bring about. But they turn, left up the hill back towards town, and I'm suddenly terrified they are about to do it all again, as if they are thinking: This time, maybe we'll find the right spot.

Acknowledgments

Thank you to my wife, Natalie, as this book would've stayed in the dusty shelves of my brain had it not been for the fifteen years of conversations we've had on the scenes herein. To my parents, Barbara and James Foote, my brother Caleb, my sister Allyson, and my in-laws Linda and Eric Robinson, who have never been anything but loving and supportive, even when that meant having pieces of their story told and published by someone else. To my friend and editor, John Dixon Mirisola, who took this project on amidst so many other more important endeavors. I feel incredibly lucky to have had access to such a talented and insightful editor and person.

The following records were absolutely critical to the way this book was written: *Tertia* by Caspian, *Eingya* by Helios, *Lambent Material* by Eluvium, *Yanqui U.X.O.* by Godspeed You! Black Emperor, and the bass line in the track "Our Breaths in Winter" by Caspian—we miss you, Chris.

Many thanks to my mentors Meredith Hall and Mark Stevick, and to my writing community at the University of New Hampshire, especially Ryan Flaherty, Katie Umans, Matthew Thompson, Julie Samara Thompson, Tom Mathe, Marla Cinilia, Meg Glasson, Rosie Forrest, Sarah Stickney, Nathan Fink, Mandy Chesley-Park, Annie Lalish, Sue Hertz, and Tom Paine.

This book was written in solitude, but art cannot exist without a community. To that end, thanks to Paul Howard, Grant Hanna, Ryan Heidorn, Ryan McDonnell, Chris Stedman, Christine Ellsmore, Maia Mattson, Neil Moloney, Susanna Young, Chris and Petra Dawson, the Glenneys, Jonathan and Marika Bennett, Toddy Burton, Pete Guinta, Oliver Goodrich, Tim Ferguson-Sauder, Jon Misarski, and the Kingdom of Beverly.

ACKNOWLEDGMENTS

To my wonderful team at Cascade, Rodney Clapp, Matthew Wimer, Christian Amondson, Amanda Wehner, and Jesselyn Ewing.

Finally, thanks to everyone mentioned in this book, very few of whom would've guessed they'd ever appear in print. Thank you for letting me reckon honestly with this expression.

Made in the USA
San Bernardino, CA
05 December 2015